"What started as a children's book that inspired children and churches alike now has developed into so much more. Kevin Horath's new book, *The Donkey Factor: Living a Life Used by God*, is transformational in the reader's life, walk, and thinking. It will open up a whole new spiritual dimension in your life. There is so much biblical insight compressed in these pages, producing a totally new insight. I have been called a lot of names in my life, and yes, jackass has been one of them, but I never realized until now what a compliment that really was. If you want to go deeper in your relationship with the Lord, don't miss this read. Change your life. Read the book."

—Pastor Keenan Smith,
Cofounder of Team Impact, Pastor of Crosby Church

"Since getting to know Kevin and his work, I increasingly admire his wit and honesty. He has a talent for highlighting the subtleties of biblical characters and how they apply to shifting cultural trends as well as firm, forever truth. *The Donkey Factor* is a fresh means to find commonality and symbolism with a seemingly stubborn, fiercely protective, faithfully loyal, and precious creature. You will be thankful you have some things in common with a donkey, and you will be surprised at the treasure God intended to show us through them. I truly appreciate Kevin's work and words in *The Donkey Factor*."

—Amberlin Harrison,
Author and blogger, amberlinbooks.com

D0937304

"A book about donkeys? For this, he went to college? I have to be honest, I wondered at first. However, I truly believe my son, Kevin P. Horath, has written a must-read devotional for anyone interested in learning more about themselves by studying donkeys. Read this book—and learn."

— **Pastor Donald E. Horath**,
Founding Pastor, Hillside Bethel Tabernacle

"This book is unlike anything you have ever read. Think about it; while we were all at work, Kevin was researching donkeys. Wow! What a life."

—**Pastor Adam Lewis**,
Lead Pastor, Decatur First Church of the Nazarene

"Kevin has done a marvelous job making an 'ass' of himself with these beasts of burden. After relating to Kevin's conversational tone of no-nonsense truth and abundant grace to all, I too want to be like Balaam's donkey, willing to take a beating for what's right to protect others. I want to carry the sign of the cross on my back like all donkeys everywhere. Talk about picking up your cross daily! Kevin, thank you for showing us how to live a life used by God. I'm in!"

—**Reverend Jennifer Ervig**,
Author of *As My Mind Unwinds* and
When My Mind Winds Up

"In Pastor Kevin's newest *Factor* book, he addresses all factors associated with the donkey—an amazing animal that most of us give very little credit to until we realize how they were used by God to fulfill various roles. *The Donkey Factor* is a well-written devotional for individuals of various spiritual maturity levels and can be utilized as a personal devotion, a small group study, or even material for pastors.

Pastor Kevin uses an honest conversational style with notorious puns throughout the book, which is guaranteed to keep any reader's attention. I highly recommend Pastor Kevin's new devotional to all believers. And as a Type A Christian who thrives on success, I love that Pastor Kevin says, "[God] is not impressed by your ability. He just wants your availability." I am forever grateful for the Lamb of God who took my place, and like Daniel the Donkey, I pray that I fulfill my purpose in carrying God's Word to others."

—Autumn Hoover,
Christian speaker and author of *Type A Christian*,
pastor's wife, mother, and women's health nurse practitioner

The Donkey Factor:
Living a Life Used by God

KEVIN P. HORATH

LUCIDBOOKS

The Donkey Factor
Living a Life Used by God

ISBN 978-1-63296-451-9 (paperback)
ISBN 978-1-63296-452-6 (ebook)

For Kathy

Thank you for believing in and helping tame this wild donkey
of a man. I love you!

Table of Contents

Foreword

I met Kevin Horath several years ago when he was a guest on my podcast. He was there to talk about a new book, a book he had written—a book about a donkey.

I was intrigued as you would be about his new book. I mean, come on! A book about a donkey? That's probably the same thought you had when you purchased this book, right?

The Bible is not a pick-and-choose kind of book. If we really sift through its content, we will find the big, well-known pieces of God's Word—the ones we are always talking about, preaching on, and sharing with others. In that sifting, there are a few smaller pieces left for us to consider. One of those pieces is the role of God's animals, more specifically, the donkey.

I'm sure there are times in Kevin's life when he has been told to stop—stop bothering his sibling, stop singing an annoying song, stop telling his dad-jokes. No matter his response to those times, Kevin stopped for this book. He stopped at several spots in God's Word and decided to dig deeper into the significance of this animal that we knew was there for a reason but never really cared enough to figure out what that reason was.

Never in my life would I think that a book about a donkey would actually be about me. Yes, I said that (stop with the jokes—Kevin's got plenty in the chapters ahead). A book about a donkey is actually a book that convicts me to be a better messenger of God's Word. A book about a donkey is actually a book that challenges me to tame my own selfish desires. A book about a donkey is a book that reminds me of my own redemption in Christ. Through the pages of Kevin's research and insight, you will see how powerful and creative God has been. God can even use a donkey to speak to us.

Kevin's goal in this book is to connect us to the elements of God's story, no matter how large, furry, or smelly. These elements are the ones that are significant enough to tell our story.

When you are finished, you will agree that this book is unlike anything you have ever read. Think about it. While we were all at work, Kevin was researching donkeys. Wow! What a life!

—Pastor Adam Lewis
Lead Pastor, Decatur First Church of the Nazarene

Introduction

Rejoice greatly, O daughter of Zion; shout, O daughter of Jerusalem: behold, thy King cometh unto thee: he is just, and having salvation; lowly, and riding upon an ass, and upon a colt the foal of an ass.

—Zech. 9:9

A couple of years ago I was scheduled to preach on Palm Sunday. Because it is a significant religious day and celebration, I felt somewhat obligated to have a sermon with a foundation of this particular event. It is just normal protocol and kind of expected, I guess. Growing up in church, I have heard the story all my life and thought I knew it pretty well. It is absolutely a great event, and the story stands on its own merits. It really doesn't need a new meaning. However, I was looking for a way to come at it from a different angle. I guess I wanted something fresh, a new perspective.

But what could that perspective be? The story has been told so many times. What could I find that was new? Of course, I knew the basic premise. I had heard sermons and teachings over the years that compared and contrasted the attitudes of the people. On Palm Sunday they cried out to Jesus, "Hosanna to the son of David: Blessed is he that cometh in the name of the Lord" (Matt.

21:9). A few days later they cried, "Crucify him" (Mark 15:13, 14). What a dichotomy! What a change in just a few short days! Why did that occur? How did it happen? Were the people really that wishy-washy? If so, how does that apply to us today? While these were good thoughts and worthy of investigation, they weren't enough for me this time around. I wanted something more.

So I researched the story more than I had before. What I discovered caused me to divert my attention from the people to Jesus. In doing so, I became convinced that it was not necessarily the same crowd who had cheered for Jesus on Sunday; these were different people who were railing on Him now. I believe something significant happened. The focus of the story should not be about our fickleness. The focus rightly should be on Jesus. And I discovered that this story is, indeed, also about us. It is not about us when we look at the actions and reactions of the people that day, but it is about us when we see the characteristics of an important yet sometimes overlooked side character in the story—the donkey.

The prophet Zechariah had prophesized that Jesus would ride into Jerusalem on a donkey. But why did Jesus have to ride on a donkey? We often juxtapose Jesus's humble entry with kings and warriors riding majestically and fearlessly on great horses. And instead of an imposing presentation of power, Jesus rides on a lowly donkey while making His triumphal entry into Jerusalem. Was this simply to fulfill prophecy, or is there something else happening here that we need to know?

I thought there had to be more. And there was. As I investigated further, I learned that donkeys were used as a common mode of transportation for just about everyone. People of all backgrounds and professions, including people of great importance, rode donkeys. Prophets, priests, and kings regularly rode donkeys. In fact, I was surprised to learn that King Solomon made a similar entrance into Jerusalem when he was anointed king.

And king David said, Call me Zadok the priest, and Nathan the prophet, and Benaiah the son of Jehoiada. And they came before the king. The king also said unto them, Take with you the servants of your lord, and cause Solomon my son to ride upon mine own mule, and bring him down to Gihon: And let Zadok the priest and Nathan the prophet anoint him there king over Israel: and blow ye with the trumpet, and say, God save king Solomon. Then ye shall come up after him, that he may come and sit upon my throne; for he shall be king in my stead: and I have appointed him to be ruler over Israel and over Judah.

—1 Kings 1:32–35

While Solomon rode his dad's old mule (the offspring between a male donkey and a female horse), Jesus rode on a purebred donkey, one that had never been ridden before. Jesus's entry into Jerusalem was slightly different, yet the people probably would not have considered it all that unusual for a king. In fact, it was expected. But that is only part of the story. While we rightly read Zechariah 9:9 today as a messianic promise of Jesus, we often stop there and do not examine the next few verses.

And I will cut off the chariot from Ephraim, and the horse from Jerusalem, and the battle bow shall be cut off: and he shall speak peace unto the heathen: and his dominion shall be from sea even to sea, and from the river even to the ends of the earth. As for thee also, by the blood of thy covenant I have sent forth thy prisoners out of the pit wherein is no water.

—Zech. 9:10–11

I don't know about you, but I find this to be a stunning oracle. In it, the future king (Jesus) not only rides into Jerusalem on a donkey in humility, but He also establishes a universal kingdom ("to the ends of the earth"). This king is characterized by peace, not war (the chariot is cut off), and His kingdom is in force through the power of a blood covenant. If this doesn't get a preacher ready to preach, I don't know what will. For through the blood covenant, God sets the captive free from the waterless pit, or Sheol, which is the realm of the dead. Zechariah clearly expected the messianic return from exile to include those who had died, descended into Sheol, and would be released through the "blood of thy covenant." This is not just a physical redemption or deliverance of Israel by means of an earthly kingdom. It is a spiritual one. This prophecy shows that the sacrificial death of Jesus is for all people for all time—even those who died in faith before Christ.

What a powerful prophecy and powerful imagery!

That is the message of the triumphal entry. Entirely missed by the crowds (and many today), it was heralding the upcoming work of the cross. That is the core message of Palm Sunday. However, I did not want to stop there. I wanted to dig deeper into the role of the donkey and its part in the story. We generally only refer to the donkey as a humble alternative to a horse. And that's good, but I needed to know whether the symbolism was more complex than that. So I began a journey into the world of the donkey and specifically the world of the donkey as referenced throughout the Bible. What I discovered amazed me. It was right before my eyes the whole time, but I had never made the connection—until now. And I want to share this revelation with you.

The donkey is representative of us.

It's true. And the humor is not lost on me, especially as I read and study from the King James Version of the Bible. I use a lot of translations, but I generally use the King James Version as my foundational text. It is what I have studied and memorized the most. Therefore, it flows much easier in my mind, in my speech, and in my writing.

It also presents a few challenges. Unfortunately, language and words change over time. So let's go ahead and address it. Let's get it out of the way. We all know the original English term for a donkey, right? The King James Version uses that term, and we all giggle and snicker when we say it. We laugh like school kids because as we read it, we are allowed to say a "bad" word. Come on! Be honest. Who hasn't laughed when it was read aloud?

The preacher said "ass" [giggle, snort].

If you study etymology (the study of the origin of words and the way their meanings have changed throughout history), you will learn something about the donkey. The original and, I dare say, proper English term is *ass*, and it refers to the animal we call a donkey today. Unfortunately, this original term sounded like another term that describes part of the anatomy. Because of this similarity, the lexicon changed the meaning of *ass* to a vulgar term and something totally different than its original meaning.

Why do I share this? Because it is important in order to understand the Bible. We must understand words, realizing that meanings change over time. Therefore, we have to be careful. If we use the word as it was originally intended, it is not really cursing. However, we have become sensitive to the sounds of words rather than their original meaning. We sometimes find it difficult to talk about these things because people can be offended by the sound of a word they hear (like *ass*) rather than the actual meaning behind it (pun intended).

Are you with me so far? I hope so. Let's keep going because I want us to understand some other terms. For many years, *ass* and *she-ass* were completely normal and accepted terms that people used to describe their pack animals. Additionally, a jack is a male donkey, and a ginny is a female donkey. Today, however, to call someone a jackass is offensive because it is calling that person stubborn, obnoxious, or even stupid. We might try to be polite and call someone a stubborn mule or a stupid donkey instead, but in reality we are saying the same thing. It is still offensive. We are just using words that are less offensive *sounding*.

Regardless, it is still a fallacy no matter our intent or what term for donkey we use to insult someone. For some reason, the donkey is considered stupid when, in fact, it is really quite intelligent. This reminds of me of a popular video game I used to play when I was a kid. It was called *Donkey Kong*. Remember that video game? I wasn't very good at it, but I loved it. I played it every chance I got. I never quite understood why the name of the game was *Donkey Kong*, but that didn't matter to me. I played it anyway.

While researching donkeys and this particular topic, I came across some information about this game. Because I loved it so much, it piqued my interest. I took what I thought was a little detour from my studies and learned that the Japanese makers of the game thought *Kong* meant "gorilla" and *Donkey* meant "stupid" because of how these words were used in American popular culture. The antagonist of the video game is a character not unlike King Kong. Therefore, the makers of the game thought they were saying "stupid gorilla." It didn't involve a donkey at all. Something got lost in translation.

I think that happens in our language, too. Unfortunately, donkeys have gotten a bad rap. If you conduct a search on the Internet, you will quickly find that donkeys are exceptionally intelligent animals. They have great memories and can recall complex routes and recognize animals they haven't seen for years. They are even able to solve problems by using a form of logic. Pound for pound, donkeys are stronger than horses. In addition to being smart and strong, they are known to be personable and affectionate.

When I say the Bible uses donkeys as representative of us, that is not an insult. As you take a look at *The Donkey Factor*, I hope you will come to realize that, too. I also want our children to recognize this. During the process of learning about donkeys in the Bible and preaching a sermon series on this topic, a children's story came to me. I was able to publish a children's book about these events called *Daniel and the Donkey Factor*. My desire is for this adult book to serve as a companion guide to the children's book. In this book, we will explore the themes and concepts from *Daniel and the Donkey Factor* in much more depth.

Here is a fair warning, though. I am going to have some fun with it. Please do not get offended. Realize that I am using the original meaning of the word and maybe some, ahem, cheeky humor, too.

See what I just did there?

Oh yeah, and I want you to remember this. The next time someone calls you a jackass, be sure to thank them. Yep. It's quite the compliment. You don't believe me just yet? Well, stay with me. I am sure you will by the time you are finished.

Thanks for joining me as we study *The Donkey Factor: Living a Life Used by God*.

Factor One
A Wild Donkey of a Man

And he will be a wild man; his hand will be against
every man, and every man's hand against him; and he
shall dwell in the presence of all his brethren.
—Gen. 16:12

As we established in the Introduction, the donkey is a very versa-tile, trusted animal. What has become a derogatory term today is really not accurate. However, we do find early on in Scripture that the Bible uses the donkey as a way to describe various individuals. One of the first examples is in Genesis 16:12 where Ishmael, the son of Abraham and Hagar, is described as a "wild donkey of a man" (NIV).

In this verse, the King James Version does not use the term *ass.* It simply calls Ishmael a wild man. By not using the term *ass* here, we can easily miss something very important and therefore misunderstand what the Bible is telling us. Ishmael was not merely a wild man. When you compare this verse with other translations (e.g., NIV), you will find that Ishmael is called "a wild donkey of a man." In other words, Ishmael was a wild jackass.

In today's terminology, that certainly would be considered an insult, maybe even fighting words. But remember, donkeys have great characteristics. The term is not the insult we might think. In fact, the book of Job, perhaps the oldest book in the Bible that was no doubt written even before Genesis, uses a wild donkey as an illustration of the greatness of God.

> *Who hath sent out the wild ass free? or who hath loosed the bands of the wild ass? Whose house I have made the wilderness, and the barren land his dwellings. He scorneth the multitude of the city, neither regardeth he the crying of the driver. The range of the mountains is his pasture, and he searcheth after every green thing.*
>
> —Job 39:5–8

A wild donkey is unruly and untamed. While an amazing creature and a beautiful part of God's creation, it is not very purposeful when left in that state. Although impressive in nature, the wild donkey is not very beneficial to anyone. At its worst, it can be a nuisance and quite destructive. However, when domesticated, just the opposite occurs. The tame donkey becomes very useful and practical.

Just like us.

Many of us love to celebrate our wild side. We love that thing that makes us feel like a man or a woman, and we revel in it. I guess I can understand that and to a certain extent, I even agree with doing it. However, while God created us and we all have these amazing characteristics we can celebrate, He does not mean for us to remain wild in our sin nature. He wants to tame our hearts. Ishmael's problem was not that he was a jackass or a donkey of a man; his problem was that he remained wild at heart. He needed taming. When we remain wild, we are not very useful. We are destructive. Sin destroys everything around us. It will eventually destroy us, too.

I know there have been recent trends of celebrating our gender-specific characteristics, even in the midst of our Christianity. Although there is neither male nor female in Christ (Gal. 3:28), we often celebrate the power of our gender. Books have been written. Groups have been formed. Conferences have been held. Men do it. So do women. I am not advocating that we completely abandon what defines us. It is God-given. I just believe we must allow God to tame that wild spirit within us, especially as it involves our sin nature. Don't simply celebrate it or excuse it away. Your acceptance of yourself in that state is not good enough. You must allow God to tame you.

Unfortunately, we often don't want to hear that. To be tamed may seem like emasculation to a man. To a woman, it may feel like she is put under submission and held back from her full potential. To those struggling with their identity (sexually or otherwise), it may seem like they are simply made that way and the acceptance of such is the pathway to true freedom. All of us in some way or another may think taming ourselves will rob us of our identity, make us weaker or less effective versions of ourselves, or even place us in a state of bondage. We could not be more wrong.

When someone's spirit is broken, we often equate that to depression, addictions, compulsive behaviors, and low self-esteem. It sounds awful and not desirable at all. Therefore, in the natural, we don't want to be broken. Yet that is the very thing God desires. "The sacrifices of God are a broken spirit: a broken and a contrite heart, O God, thou wilt not despise" (Ps. 51:17).

To have a contrite spirit means we feel guilt or remorse over our wrongdoing. It means we seek repentance in place of our sin and rebellion. However, repentance does not end with us sitting in guilt and shame forever. Repentance does not mean we have low self-esteem or no confidence in Christ. True repentance brings us into the joy of His salvation and sets us on the right track of following

Him. Instead of going our own way, wild and free like the feral donkey, we are tamed and useful when we are broken before God.

Being tame—being broken—does not mean we are weak. We have to stop that kind of thinking. Like many things in Scripture, this concept is a paradox. Brokenness is actually a sign of strength. "When I am weak, then I am strong" (2 Cor. 12:10). One of the great patriarchs in the Old Testament, Jacob, gave a prophecy and blessing over his sons just before he died. Genesis 49 records his words, and I found them fascinating and demonstrative.

> *Issachar is a strong ass couching down between two burdens: And he saw that rest was good, and the land that it was pleasant; and bowed his shoulder to bear, and became a servant unto tribute.*
>
> —Gen. 49:14–15

Donkeys serve. It is what they do. Even when resting, they provide an important function. Donkeys are often turned out to pasture with cattle or other livestock to protect them from predators. I noticed that some translations refer to the "two burdens" as two sheepfolds. That makes sense because donkeys work hard doing their jobs as beasts of burden, and they are also fiercely protective of the herd.

Issachar's blessing was to be an ass, protecting the rest of the flock. He was strong and robust, able to carry burdens. He served, bowed, protected, and performed hard work. To do this, he had to be tamed. But he was still strong. He was an ass in the truest sense of the word, not for stupidity or sluggishness but for his strength and integrity.

A few verses later, we find Jacob's blessing that he gave to Joseph. "Joseph is a fruitful bough, even a fruitful bough by a well; whose branches run over the wall" (Gen. 49:22).

Wait a minute. What does that have to do with a donkey? While many translations read like the King James Version printed here, some newer translations such as the New Living Translation call Joseph the "foal of a wild donkey" and "one of the wild donkeys on the ridge." That is different than being called a fruitful bough or a fruitful vine. Much different.

If this newer translation is a more accurate reflection of the original text and meaning, and I believe it could be, what is Jacob actually telling us about Joseph? Perhaps the foundation of its meaning goes back to the day when Joseph was sold by his brothers into slavery.

> *Then there passed by Midianites merchantmen; and they drew and lifted up Joseph out of the pit, and sold Joseph to the Ishmeelites for twenty pieces of silver: and they brought Joseph into Egypt.*
>
> —Gen. 37:28

There was obviously some hostility among Joseph and his brothers. They sold him into slavery, and Joseph came under the control and subsequent influence of the Ishmaelites, who were the direct descendants of Ishmael. Remember what was said about Ishmael? It is how we started this chapter.

> *He will be a wild donkey of a man;*
> *his hand will be against everyone*
> *and everyone's hand against him,*
> *and he will live in hostility*
> *toward all his brothers.*
>
> —Gen. 16:12 (NIV)

Perhaps this is a direct link to Ishmael in Jacob's blessing to Joseph. Maybe it was due to the family feud among Jacob's sons. It was brother against brother. Just how much of the Ishmaelite way actually rubbed off on Joseph in captivity? In my opinion, probably not too much. Although Joseph was deemed a wild donkey because of the contention with his brothers, he learned how to overcome the hostility that occurred among them. He learned how to be tamed. God was then able to use him to save all of Israel in the time of famine. Joseph refused to go the way of Ishmael, even though he had every reason and excuse in the natural to do so. Instead, his wild heart was tamed. It was tamed by God, and he became a man of strength and integrity.

Perhaps another good example in Scripture is Peter, one of the twelve disciples and an early apostle. He was quite impulsive and wild. If anyone anywhere was considered wild at heart, it was Peter. It would be safe to call him a wild jackass. He was quick to act and react. He was even known to overreact. I think it is fair to say that he had a big mouth, and it often got him in all kinds of trouble.

But once Peter truly repented after he denied Jesus, he was restored in his relationship with the Lord. After he was filled with the Spirit on the Day of Pentecost, God was able to tame his heart and his tongue. It was then that Peter preached one of the most powerful sermons ever recorded. You can find it in Acts 2. When we are broken before God, we have access to a power far greater than we could ever imagine, even though we may consider ourselves wild and strong on our own.

If God could tame Peter's heart and use his big mouth, He can do the same with ours.

The donkey was, and is, an important animal throughout history and in biblical times. I don't think it was a coincidence that Jesus used this animal. Its characteristics—both good and bad—apply to us today. We can be feral and demonstrate the natural characteristics of a wild donkey, untamed by mankind. Or we can be domesticated and broken, available to be used by God for His purposes. "But the tongue can no man tame; it is an unruly evil, full of deadly poison" (James 3:8).

> *Because that he had been often bound with fetters and chains, and the chains had been plucked asunder by him, and the fetters broken in pieces: neither could any man tame him.*
>
> —Mark 5:4

> *Come unto me, all ye that labour and are heavy laden, and I will give you rest. Take my yoke upon you, and learn of me; for I am meek and lowly in heart: and ye shall find rest unto your souls. For my yoke is easy, and my burden is light.*
>
> —Matt. 11:28–30

Instead of being a wild jackass, we should want to be a strong ass, tamed and used by God. We will see in the next chapter that God used the tongue of a tamed donkey in a miraculous way.

Factors to Consider

1. How do you react when someone calls you a bad name or uses a derogatory term?

2. Can you be wild at heart and tamed by God at the same time? Why or why not?

3. What does it mean to have a broken and contrite heart? Why is it important?

4. What are some of your characteristics that, when tamed, can be used by God? What is the result of remaining untamed?

5. What are some ways you can serve and protect those around you?

Factor Two

A Mad Prophet and a Talking Donkey

And when the ass saw the angel of the Lord, she fell down under Balaam: and Balaam's anger was kindled, and he smote the ass with a staff.

—Num. 22:27

As I studied the many characteristics of donkeys, I discovered that they are not easily startled. They have a keen sense of curiosity, but they also have a high sense of self-preservation. That is probably why they have a reputation for stubbornness, for it is very difficult to force a donkey to do something it sees as contrary to its own best interest of safety.

Horses, on the other hand, are different. I am not an equestrian or an experienced horseback rider, but I did take our family riding a few years ago in Texas. It was right after Hurricane Harvey, and we went to the Houston area to visit family. Cleanup was happening all across the region, including the area around the stables we visited.

Although much had already been cleaned up when we arrived, there was still a lot of visible devastation. When we went horseback riding, we followed a trail that took us along Spring Creek, a winding river in Humble, Texas. Even with the damage from the storm, it was still beautiful country. I love Texas, and when in Texas, you have to ride horses, right?

As we were riding, men operating some heavy equipment and machinery were cleaning debris along the riverbank. Suddenly, a log snapped loudly in two, and the sound echoed through the trees. That spooked our horses, which nearly turned into a very serious problem. My son was ahead of me, and I was immediately concerned for his safety because the horses just about took off in a hard run. It was my son's first time on a horse, and I knew he didn't know what to do. I know I sure didn't. Thankfully, our guide knew exactly how to handle the situation, and he was able to quickly and safely calm our horses. I have to admit, my heart was racing for just a few scary moments.

I have always heard that horses spook easily, and I experienced it firsthand that day. Donkeys, though, do not. They take a more measured response to situations happening around them. Instead of running away at full speed, they stop and consider their options. When threatened, they tend to freeze. They do not act upon a hasty impulse or instinct that will lead to more danger. And that leads us to a perfect example in Scripture.

When I think about donkeys in the Bible, two main stories come to mind. The first, which we have already talked about, is Palm Sunday. The second is the story of Balaam's donkey. If you have ever attended Sunday school, I am sure you have heard about this incident. As much as I heard this story growing up, I was amazed at how little of the story I actually knew. I mean, this story is great for Sunday school. It has talking donkeys! What more do you need? Apparently, a lot more as I soon discovered.

And the ass said unto Balaam, Am not I thine ass, upon which thou hast ridden ever since I was thine unto this day? was I ever wont to do so unto thee? and he said, Nay.

—Num. 22:30

It is no wonder I never fully understood this story. Everything is turned around. We have donkeys that talk like humans. We have humans sounding like horses (Balaam said, nay; the sound of a horse is written neigh—oh, never mind). Anyway, it's all mixed up, and it is, quite frankly, a bit confusing. Just what is the significance of this story anyway?

Let's break it down.

The story of Balaam begins in Numbers 22 in the Bible. From a time line perspective, the events occurred during the journey of the Israelites through the desert and across the plains of Moab. They were just east of the Jordan River at the close of their 40 years of wandering. In the context of other major events, this story happened just before the death of Moses and the Israelites' subsequent crossing of the Jordan River into the Promised Land.

At this point, the Israelites had already defeated two kings. Word was getting out about this mass of people crossing the desert, led by a cloud by day and fire by night. It must have been a sight to behold. Other kings in the area were starting to get a little concerned, and rightly so. Israel was rapidly gaining a reputation. Balak, king of Moab, became alarmed because the Israelites were knocking on his door. In response, he sent messengers to Balaam, son of Beor, to try to induce him to come and pronounce a curse upon Israel. Balak was trying to avoid being conquered and was willing to try just about anything.

To his credit, Balaam, who was a prophet, sent word back to Balak that he could only do what God commanded. In a dream, God told Balaam not to go, so Balaam would not go. Simple. Balak, however, would not be easily deterred. In order to persuade Balaam, Balak sent princes in an attempt to bribe him to come and curse Israel. That must have been appealing to Balaam because he continued to press God on the issue, and God finally permitted him to go under one condition. Even then, Balaam was under strict instructions to say only what God commanded.

> *And God came unto Balaam at night, and said unto him, If the men come to call thee, rise up, and go with them; but yet the word which I shall say unto thee, that shalt thou do. And Balaam rose up in the morning, and saddled his ass, and went with the princes of Moab.*
> —Num. 22:20–21

So Balaam went. However, this made God extremely angry. In Numbers 22:22, we see that in response, God sent the angel of the Lord to stop him from going.

Let's pause right there for a moment. Why did God get angry with Balaam? Didn't He say that Balaam could go? I don't know about you, but this seems like a setup. God is not playing fairly. Or is He? Read carefully the conditions under which Balaam could go in Numbers 22:20. Then read what actually happened in Numbers 22:21.

If you didn't catch it, here it is. I will show you. God's first word in His response to Balaam is critical. It is only two letters, but it is very powerful. The word is *if.* This word describes God's response, which is a conditional statement—"If the men come to call thee, rise up, and go with them" (Num. 22:20). If this happens, then do that. Nowhere in the text do we see that Balaam satisfied the condition God set. The *if* didn't happen. Therefore, the *then* should not have happened. Balaam should not have gone.

If I understand God's instructions correctly, it appears He intended for Balaam to wait for the princes to come to Balaam's tent in the morning to inquire after God's will. To be sure, this would have been a humbling experience for them. It would have demonstrated to everyone that God—not Balak—was the ultimate authority regarding blessings and curses. And it certainly wasn't Balaam who, to me, seemed just a little too eager to go and do this thing.

In light of 2 Peter 2:15 and Jude 1:11, it is likely that Balaam's greedy desire for profit from the Moabites would have shown itself as his eagerness to go with them. Balaam was trying to find a way, any possible way, to go, even if that meant finding a loophole. I think he desperately wanted the honors and riches that Balak had promised. His greed became his downfall. He tried to make his own wants and desires happen, even ahead of God's. He tried to find a way to technically speak God's words. He kept the letter of the Law but ignored its spirit, wanting to play the other side. Yeah, I guess you could say he was a double agent.

> *Which have forsaken the right way, and are gone astray, following the way of Balaam the son of Bosor, who loved the wages of unrighteousness.*
>
> —2 Pet. 2:15

> *Woe unto them! For they have gone in the way of Cain, and ran greedily after the error of Balaam for reward, and perished in the gainsaying of Core.*
>
> —Jude 1:11

Balaam, blinded by his own greed, got up on his own and went with the princes. He didn't obey God with the first condition because he didn't wait for the men to come to him. I believe this is what angered God. Disobedience. As a result, God sent an angel to intervene. But this was not just any ordinary angel (sorry, Clarence). This was the angel of the Lord. It was a theophany. More specifically, it was a Christophany—a pre-Bethlehem manifestation of Jesus. And when Jesus showed up, things began to happen.

At first, the donkey was the only one that saw the angel of the Lord. Three times the donkey tried to avoid the angel, but Balaam tried to press on. He didn't know what was happening. Remember the characteristics of the donkey we talked about at the beginning of this chapter? While curious, a donkey will not do anything it deems dangerous or put its own safety in jeopardy. Not understanding, Balaam assumed (and you know what happens when we assume, right?) that his donkey was just being stubborn. He punished her with a beating. He beat his ass.

After the beatings began, God miraculously gave the donkey the power of speech. She complained about Balaam's treatment of her, and at that point, Balaam was also allowed to see the angel of the Lord. The Lord quickly informed Balaam that the donkey was the only reason He did not kill Balaam. Avoiding the angel and stopping in her tracks, the donkey had unwittingly saved Balaam's life. And what did Balaam do? He beat the donkey. But once he recognized what had actually happened, he immediately repented. God told Balaam to proceed but to only speak the words God gave him.

There is a lot more to this story, and it can be difficult putting all the pieces together. While Balaam did bless Israel three times as the word of the Lord had instructed, he was also able to manipulate the situation and find a way to curse Israel. As a result, Balaam eventually lost his own life. God takes it very seriously when someone actively participates in causing His own to stumble. Very. Seriously.

> *But I have a few things against thee, because thou hast there them that hold the doctrine of Balaam, who taught Balac to cast a stumblingblock before the children of Israel, to eat things sacrificed unto idols, and to commit fornication.*
>
> —Rev. 2:14

Balaam thought he could technically obey God and still get what he wanted, no matter whom it hurt. He was incorrect. With God's protection taken from him, Balaam was listed among the Midianites who were killed in revenge for the matter of Peor. Numbers 31:8 records that Balaam died by the sword during a battle for the Reubanite occupation of Moabite land. He got his reward.

Now what exactly did Balaam do to deserve this? I am not sure of all the specific details. The Bible doesn't really tell us. However, Numbers 25:1–9 describes how Israel engaged in sexual immorality and idolatry with the women of Moab, resulting in God's anger and a deadly plague. If we read further, we find that Numbers 31:16 traces this sin back to Balaam's advice.

> Behold, these caused the children of Israel, through
> the counsel of Balaam, to commit trespass against the
> LORD in the matter of Peor, and there was a plague
> among the congregation of the LORD.
>
> —Num. 31:16

I am not sure what counsel Balaam gave Balak, but whatever it was, it worked. Instead of a payoff to Balaam, it ultimately came at a great cost to him. Had Balaam bridled his greediness instead of immediately bridling his donkey to go with the men, he would have saved himself some embarrassment and perhaps even his life. He could have arguably saved Israel a lot of trouble, too. Instead, he brought death and destruction to everyone around him.

What can we learn from Balaam and his talking donkey? Some say that Balaam simply got ahead of God and tried to make things happen on his own. Getting ahead of God is never good. That much is true. However, I think this story is much more than that. Balaam didn't just try to get ahead of God. He tried to serve both God and mammon, which was actually contrary to God the whole time. He had a wrong motive.

*No man can serve two masters: for either he will hate
the one, and love the other; or else he will hold to the
one, and despise the other. Ye cannot serve God and
mammon.*

—Matt. 6:24

Despite all this, the donkey tried to get Balaam's attention by demonstrating there was trouble ahead. When that didn't work, God used the donkey to literally speak to Balaam, but Balaam just wouldn't listen. Although somewhat repentant, Balaam still thought he could be manipulative and get what he wanted.

That did not keep the donkey from doing her job. Even after being beaten, she was faithful. She looked to Jesus. She saw. She obeyed. She knew that danger would befall them if they kept going the way they were headed. Conversely, Balaam was blinded by his own greediness. He was a seer, yet he couldn't see. A prophet, Balaam was more interested in making a profit.

*Not every one that saith unto me, Lord, Lord, shall
enter into the kingdom of heaven; but he that doeth the
will of my Father which is in heaven. Many will say to
me in that day, Lord, Lord, have we not prophesied in
thy name? and in thy name have cast out devils? and
in thy name done many wonderful works? And then
will I profess unto them, I never knew you: depart from
me, ye that work iniquity.*

—Matt. 7:21–23

We will learn more about the typology of donkeys and prophets in the next chapter. Despite what I am about to say, I want you to understand that I believe prophets are important today. Prophecy is a vital gift of the Spirit in the church, and I am so thankful for that. I know there are a lot of prophets today declaring the Word of God.

However, while some may be saying the right things, I believe many have abandoned the right way. These prophets are seeking their own gain—money, power, popularity, politics, and influence—but, like Balaam, they can't see Jesus. Many are seeking earthly success instead of eternal rewards and not really caring who is hurt in the process. They have gone the way of Balaam.

I know I am having some fun with this topic, and it is okay to have fun. But let me be very serious for a moment. The problem with Balaam was greed. That greed caused him to negatively influence and entrap Israel. That does not take the responsibility of Israel's sin away from them. They should have known better. However, the one who is implicit in causing another to stumble is in a precarious situation.

> *But whoso shall offend one of these little ones which*
> *believe in me, it were better for him that a millstone*
> *were hanged about his neck, and that he were drowned*
> *in the depth of the sea.*
>
> —Matt. 18:6

At the writing of this book in 2020, the political climate in the United States is severely divided. For the most part, evangelicals threw their political weight behind a party and candidate they thought was best for the country. In many cases, I think they also did what they thought was best for their own ministry. The year 2020 was fraught with politics and a pandemic. In the middle of it, I saw prophets who, like Balaam, heard from God. They did. But also, like Balaam, many of them saw an opportunity for personal gain and influence. And people fell for it. Hard.

My own personal politics aside, I have preached for years the danger of placing our patriotism on the same or higher level than our Christianity. Unfortunately, I think many in the church idolized President Trump too much. There, I said it. Many prophets encouraged this idolization by their words, predictions, and incessant questioning how anyone could be a Christian and vote for any other candidate.

The mad, fever-pitch of an American gospel was louder than the gospel of Christ. There were veiled (or maybe not so veiled) threats to touch not the Lord's anointed. Even disobedience to those in authority over perceived persecutions was encouraged. If you didn't obey these prophets, you were called a faithless pansy as they screamed and yelled with their so-called righteous indignation. Seriously? Talk about the madness of the prophet! The last time I checked, my salvation was based solely on faith in Jesus Christ, not my vote on the election ballot. Furthermore, unless I am told not to preach Jesus or otherwise violate Scripture, I believe I am commanded to obey those in authority. Period.

Did these prophets go the way of Balaam as the Bible warns against by encouraging the church to participate in a form of idolatry and spiritual adultery? I know it is not popular, and I know many will challenge me, but I think this was, in fact, the case. Just as Balaam sought earthly gain through manipulating Israel into idolatry and adultery, just as the people on Palm Sunday were cheering Jesus because they thought He was a king who would overthrow Rome and set up an earthly kingdom, the evangelical Christian put too much faith in a then-current President and presidential candidate whom they thought would be their savior, God's anointed, and thus protect their American (Christian?) way of life.

That's tough. I know. It's also pretty general, and I am painting with a fairly broad brush. I get that. From my humble perspective, however, it is also spot on. As I spoke against these things in real time, I realized that many found my objections to what was happening offensive and maybe even un-American. They did not want to hear it and would not accept what I had to say. Some unfriended or stopped following me on social media. Some simply ignored me.

Some questioned my faith and my patriotism, which I believe are both appropriately strong, thank you very much. However, I am sure some thought I was quite the jackass.

I hope I was.

I hope I was, and I hope I am because we need more donkeys who are faithful to carry the Word of God, to see Jesus, and to speak the truth. We need donkeys to carry the prophetic word. However, we also need donkeys who will stop us when we are headed for certain destruction. We need donkeys to stop the madness of the prophets when it occurs. We need donkeys that will even be willing to take a beating for it. It is not popular, but we need a lot more donkeys.

There is more to come on this topic. Much more. I am sure I have stirred up enough for now. As you think about these things, remember this verse:

> But was rebuked for his iniquity: the dumb ass speaking
> with man's voice forbad the madness of the prophet.
> —2 Pet. 2:16

What do we learn here? It's fairly simple. Don't be a mad prophet. Be a dumb ass.

Factors to Consider

1. How do you normally react in dangerous or scary situations?

2. What is prophecy?

3. Does prophecy occur today? If so, how do we know whether it is truly from God?

4. If you believe a prophecy is false or that a prophet is going the wrong way, what is the best way to respond? What if they don't listen?

5. Do you think evangelicals in the United States are guilty of promoting an American gospel instead of the gospel of Christ? Why or why not? If so, how do we fix this?

Factor Three
Redeeming the Beast of Burden

The burden which Habakkuk the prophet did see.
—Hab. 1:1

Although we saw differently with Balaam, true prophets of God are no triflers. They don't mess around. Isaiah, Jeremiah, Ezekiel, Elijah, Elisha, and all the major and minor prophets carried a burden. They meant business because what they carried was worth carrying— namely, the Word of God. The same is true today. Those who speak for God must not speak lightly. Even Balaam understood that part of the responsibility. God's servants, who are burdened with His Word, willingly and cheerfully carry that burden. It is a burden, but it is not burdensome.

For my yoke is easy, and my burden is light.
—Matt. 11:30

As we have discovered, the metaphorical and spiritual analogy of the donkey is an important factor. As we examine the characteristics and use of this animal, we will truly begin to understand more about ourselves. The biblical donkey represents the medium by which messages of God were delivered to the people. We saw this in the events surrounding Palm Sunday. We saw this with Balaam. In this chapter, we will investigate this thought a step further. We will see how a donkey can be in a position to be used of God in the first place.

> *And every firstling of an ass thou shalt redeem with a lamb; and if thou wilt not redeem it, then thou shalt break his neck: and all the firstborn of man among thy children shalt thou redeem.*
>
> —Exod. 13:13

> *But the firstling of an ass thou shalt redeem with a lamb: and if thou redeem him not, then shalt thou break his neck. All the firstborn of thy sons thou shalt redeem. And none shall appear before me empty.*
>
> —Exod. 34:20

Under the Law of Moses, the firstborn of cattle and sheep were offered to God. Because they were considered clean animals, they were an acceptable sacrifice. A donkey, however, was unclean. Every animal that had a split hoof not completely divided or did not chew its cud was deemed unclean. Therefore, the donkey could only be redeemed, or allowed to live, by a substitutionary sacrifice of a lamb. If a donkey was not redeemed by a lamb, the donkey was killed but not sacrificed. The context of these verses tells us that it had to do with the consecration (the setting apart for special use) of the firstborn male of every Israelite woman and every domestic animal owned by the Hebrew because of what God had done in Egypt during the tenth plague.

If you do not remember that particular story and how it all went down, you can read about it in Exodus. At the risk of making a shameless plug, I should also say that I wrote about it in *The*

Pharaoh Factor: Living with a Hardened Heart. In summary, Israel was in slavery in Egypt. Moses had delivered a message to Pharaoh many times: Let my people go! Unfortunately, Pharaoh stubbornly refused. Plague after plague, he refused and hardened his heart. And then the Lord really did something. He struck dead every firstborn in Egypt, both man and animal. However, the firstborn children and animals of the Israelites were passed over if they were protected by the blood of a lamb.

That fateful night was called Passover. On the eve of Passover, each Israelite family had to slaughter a lamb and smear the blood of that lamb on the doorposts of their house. Then they ate the lamb during a ceremonial meal. When at God's command the angel of death came to strike dead every firstborn, he passed over the Israelites' homes that were protected by the blood of the lamb. But the firstborn son of every Egyptian family and every firstborn male animal belonging to the Egyptians were killed.

That next day, Pharaoh had enough. He told Moses to take the Israelites and go. And God delivered His people with a mighty hand. It is a holiday that is celebrated to this day among the Jewish people.

With this redemption, God adopted Israel as His own. He said, "All the firstborn are mine" (Num. 3:13). As a memorial of that evening when God saved Israel and destroyed Egypt, the Israelites were to devote their eldest sons to God and sacrifice the firstborn of their clean livestock. It was a symbol and a commemoration of how the Lord had brought them out of Egypt. It was truly something special—and costly.

And yet we are left with that little colt, the foal of a donkey. What does the Israelite do with it? It is a domesticated animal, and yet it cannot be sacrificed. It is unclean, so it could not be presented to the Lord. It's quite the conundrum. Every firstborn creature—man or domestic animal—must be given to the Lord. But since the donkey was unclean, should it be allowed to live and go free, or should the

Israelites simply ignore the command and keep it? Neither was an option. God did not allow any exceptions, and disobedience was not okay. The donkey was rightfully His, and yet it could not be offered to Him. The Israelites seemed to be trapped by conflicting regulations.

There were only two choices: break the unclean animal's neck, or redeem it. The donkey had to be killed, or the donkey could be saved by the substitution of a lamb in its place.

Does that sound familiar yet?

It should. That unclean animal, that donkey, is us. Like it or not, we are the ass. We are rightly the property of the Lord, the One who made us. But the problem is that because of our sins, we are unacceptable to God. Our sins make us unclean. We are unable to be used by Him. Therefore, there is only one thing to do with the unclean one: destroy it. Sin cannot be in the presence of God, and eternal separation from Him is the only remedy. Or wait! Is there another way? Can we also be redeemed by a lamb?

> *The next day John seeth Jesus coming unto him, and saith, Behold the Lamb of God, which taketh away the sin of the world.*
>
> —John 1:29

In order to live spiritually, the Lamb of God must stand in our stead. Jesus must be our substitutionary sacrifice, and that is exactly what He came to do. Otherwise, we die. It's that simple. We now know through Scripture that the spotless Lamb of God was offered once and for all at Calvary. He has redeemed us from the deadly curse of the Law and has allowed us to serve Him.

> *And there shall be no more curse: but the throne of God and of the Lamb shall be in it; and his servants shall serve him.*
>
> —Rev. 22:3

But let's go back to the Israelites who were given the command regarding the donkey. Is this really all that simple? Could it be this easy?

Think about the choice they had to make according to the stipulations of the Law. They must have wondered what to do when a firstborn male donkey was born because they had to make a choice. Which should die? The donkey or a lamb? To us, that seems like no big deal. Just pick one. But to the Israelites, that was an important decision. Which was more valuable: the lamb, a precious commodity in those days, or the donkey, a reliable beast of burden?

Should they sacrifice the lamb to redeem the donkey, or should they break the donkey's neck? The value of the two animals had to be carefully considered, compared, and contrasted. Their livelihood depended on it, and the survival of their families weighed in the balance. Whichever was deemed of lesser value at that very moment would die. No doubt, many lambs were sacrificed for the lives of donkeys. However, I have to wonder how many times it went the other way since the lamb was so valuable and critical to their way of life.

Now think about us. Surely there is no comparison between the value of our souls and the life of the Lord Jesus. It's not even close. And yet the Lamb died for us. The human, the jackass, was spared. God looked down at us and had to make a decision. Which was of more value to Him? His Son? Or us?

> *For God so loved the world, that he gave his only*
> *begotten Son, that whosoever believeth in him should*
> *not perish, but have everlasting life.*
> —John 3:16

Christ died that we—sinners bought with the blood of Jesus—may live. The blood of the Lamb was more precious than silver, gold, the finest jewels, or anything else in the universe—with one exception. God chose us. He chose you. He chose me. That precious blood bought you and me—lowly, unclean donkeys.

> *But God commendeth his love toward us, in that, while we were yet sinners, Christ died for us. Much more then, being now justified by his blood, we shall be saved from wrath through him.*
>
> —Rom. 5:8–9

The breaking of a donkey's neck is one thing, a rather small thing when compared to the wrath to come. Yet it symbolized the eternal wrath of God, the everlasting death from which Jesus Christ, the Lamb of God, has redeemed us. As the donkey was freed to serve the Israelite once the lamb was sacrificed, so are we free to serve God because the Lamb was sacrificed on the altar of the cross.

Like the donkey, we are redeemed by the Lamb.

Isn't that amazing? Have you ever considered that the donkey is a type, or symbol, of the redemption we have through Jesus? He is the Lamb of God who redeems us to eternal life by His sacrifice. This redemption allows us to live free. Yet this freedom is meant for us to be able to be used by Him. We are not free to run wild—like Ishmael. No, we are free to carry His message, His burden. We are free to carry His Word. We are free to carry Jesus!

In the Old Testament, the donkey represented the medium by which messages of God were carried. While nearly everyone used donkeys in ancient times, if you look closely, you will find this specifically to be true with prophets, priests, and kings. Let's look at a few examples.

> *Wherefore Saul sent messengers unto Jesse, and said, Send me David thy son, which is with the sheep. And Jesse took an ass laden with bread, and*

*a bottle of wine, and a kid, and sent them by David
his son unto Saul.*

—1 Sam. 16:19–20

King Saul's servants knew the Lord was with David (see 1 Sam. 16:18). So when Saul was troubled, they sent for David to help soothe him. In response, Jesse, David's dad, loaded up the donkey and sent David on an important mission. David came to Saul with a donkey that carried bread, wine, and a goat. The common food staples of bread and wine, which are also the elements of communion, represent the body and blood of Christ. Just as the donkey carried the literal body of Christ on Palm Sunday, David, via the donkey, delivered the word of God to Saul. The physical typology seen in this passage confirms what Saul's servants knew very well. The Lord was, indeed, with David, who was able to refresh the king's spirit when he was tormented. This wasn't Saul's first experience with donkeys.

*And the asses of Kish Saul's father were lost. And Kish
said to Saul his son, Take now one of the servants with
thee, and arise, go seek the asses.*

—1 Sam. 9:3

Saul was about to be appointed king. However, his father's donkeys were lost, and Saul was sent out to search for them. Saul took some help and went looking, but he couldn't find them. On the advice of his servant, Saul went to Samuel, the prophet and priest, for help. Saul was seeking the donkeys and instead found Samuel.

God had told Samuel that He would send a man for him to anoint as king. As soon as Samuel saw Saul, the Lord confirmed that he was the man to anoint. Samuel told Saul that they would eat together that day and then Samuel would tell Saul the next day what he needed to know. While Saul was worried about the donkeys and thought that was what this was all about, Samuel quickly let him know this was, in fact, about something more substantial. He put Saul's mind at ease. Saul did not have to worry about the donkeys because they were found.

> *And as for thine asses that were lost three days ago,*
> *set not thy mind on them; for they are found. And on*
> *whom is all the desire of Israel? Is it not on thee, and*
> *on all thy father's house?*
>
> —1 Sam. 9:20

It is subtle, and maybe it is a stretch. However, I see that God used the donkeys, albeit in a roundabout way, to ensure that Saul was in the right place at the right time for Samuel, the prophet, to deliver the message and anoint him king. Once again, donkeys were used in the delivery of a message.

There is one other example from the Old Testament. It is another example of a message that was sent.

> *And the children of Israel did so: and Joseph gave them*
> *wagons, according to the commandment of Pharaoh,*
> *and gave them provisions for the way. To all of them*
> *he gave each man changes of raiment; but to Benjamin*
> *he gave three hundred pieces of silver, and five changes*
> *of raiment. And to his father he sent after this manner;*
> *ten asses laden with the good things of Egypt, and ten*
> *she-asses laden with corn and bread and meat for his*
> *father by the way. So he sent his brethren away, and*
> *they departed: and he said unto them, See that ye fall*
> *not out by the way.*
>
> —Gen. 45:21–24

This was good news for Jacob. Joseph was alive, and his brothers testified that to Jacob. Even better, Joseph was governor over all

Egypt. Unfortunately, Jacob (Israel) did not believe them (Gen. 45:26). It was too good to be true. However, when Jacob saw the provisions that Joseph had sent, including the donkeys supplied with corn, bread, and meat, he believed (Gen. 45:27). Once again, we see that donkeys delivered and confirmed the message.

So what about today? As I have stated, I believe prophecy is still relevant. When Paul was writing to the church of Thessalonica, he said this:

> *Rejoice evermore. Pray without ceasing. In every thing give thanks: for this is the will of God in Christ Jesus concerning you. Quench not the Spirit. Despise not prophesyings. Prove all things; hold fast that which is good. Abstain from all appearance of evil.*
>
> —1 Thess. 5:16–22

The purposes of prophecy as one of the gifts of the Spirit are to edify, exhort, and comfort the church. In this context, prophecy is not just predications about the future. It can be foretelling. However, prophecy is also forthtelling. Anointed preaching is, in my opinion, prophecy. As such, in all its forms, prophecy should not be despised. Yet it should be proven.

In the last chapter, I came down pretty heavily on some of the prophetic words I heard during the 2020 presidential election. The reason I did is because of 1 Thessalonians 5:21. We are to "prove all things." When the words of the prophet are incorrect, they need to be addressed, properly and in love. A prophet worth listening to will, in my opinion, receive correction. A prophet will stay close to the heart of Jesus. We all should.

> *And Samuel grew, and the LORD was with him, and did let none of his words fall to the ground.*
>
> —1 Sam. 3:19

This does not mean that God is obligated to do everything the prophet says. God does not have to line up with our wants and desires. This means that when the prophet lines up with God, it will be God's words in the prophet's mouth (Isa. 51:16, Jer. 1:9). And God always keeps His word. The same principle holds true in our prayer life. When we abide in Him, His words will abide in us. Then, and only then, can we ask and it will be done. However, it requires abiding. It requires speaking and living as moved by the Holy Spirit.

> *Knowing this first, that no prophecy of the scripture is of any private interpretation. For the prophecy came not in old time by the will of man: but holy men of God spake as they were moved by the Holy Ghost.*
> —2 Pet. 1:20–21

If we do otherwise, if prophets continue to go the way of Balaam, it can easily lead to doing what Paul instructs us not to do—despise prophesyings. In my own life, I find I can easily fall into this trap when I see the abuse of prophecy. When I see prophets go the way of Balaam, I would rather simply shut it down than see people harmed. Fortunately, I have learned that is not all we should do. The correct response is to stop, stand up for truth, and take the role of the faithful donkey like we saw in the last chapter.

The other correct response is to support and carry forward the prophetic Word of God. I am thankful for men and women I know who, without a doubt, proclaim the prophetic Word of God. I have seen it in action, and therefore I cannot throw it all out just because of the abuse of a few. I cannot despise it. I want more of it. And I am encouraged when I hear it.

There are prophets today on the local, national, and worldwide level. I am sure of that. However, the best examples I can give are ones whom I have personally witnessed. While I could share several stories from my own life, there is one in particular that stands out to me. Early in my ministry, I was a worship leader. I taught occasionally, but my focus was music ministry. One year a prophetic word was spoken over me by three individuals in unrelated situations. I can name them, and I can tell you where I was when each of them said the words to me. One came from a faithful man and brother in our church. Another came from a traveling evangelist-missionary who worked closely with Native Americans and often came to our church. The last one came from a minister in my ministerial covering, the Bethel Ministerial Association. Each one of these individuals told me, "Kevin, God is calling you to preach."

I gladly received the word from them. I believed it, and it was confirmed from the mouth of three witnesses, further strengthening my faith. I accepted it, but I still tested it. Indeed, it has come true, and I am looking forward to even greater fulfillment of this prophecy. While I love music and still love to sing, I can honestly say that my passion is teaching and preaching the Word of God. I love to find the practical application in the obscure.

That does not mean it has been easy. In fact, it has been quite the opposite. It has been hard. For years, just as I thought I was on the verge of great things, I succumbed to opposition. I questioned the call because of situations. I let resistance, hostility, and antagonism cause me to feel rejection and dejection. Several times, I almost threw in the towel. I almost called it quits.

Although there were periods of healing and growth when I did not teach or preach, I found that I identified with some of Paul's feelings. I am not saying I am Paul by any stretch of the imagination, but I am empathetic to his words in 1 Corinthians.

> *For though I preach the gospel, I have nothing to glory*
> *of: for necessity is laid upon me; yea, woe is unto me, if*
> *I preach not the gospel.*
>
> —1 Cor. 9:16

It is a burden. It is a necessity. And I am simply a redeemed beast of burden—a jackass—used to carry the Word of God. It is your responsibility, too. Even if you are not in the office of prophet or preacher, and most of us are not, we still carry and support the prophetic Word. We carry the message. We take the Prophet, Priest, and King—Jesus—to our world. The things we do confirm all these things.

> *And he said unto them, Go ye into all the world, and*
> *preach the gospel to every creature.*
> —Mark 16:15

Remember that you are just an ass that has been redeemed—redeemed to carry a burden, the Word of God. You carry the message. You carry Jesus to the people around you.

It's time for beast mode, for you are a beast of burden.

Factors to Consider

1. What was the symbolism of the Passover?

2. Jesus said that His burden is light. Do you find it easy or difficult to carry the Word of God to others? Explain your answer.

3. Have you ever had a prophetic word spoken over you? Explain how it happened. Did it come true? How did it make you feel?

4. We are instructed not to despise prophesying. How does prophecy occur in your church community?

5. Can people who are not in a formal office of pastor or prophet still preach or prophesy? Why or why not?

Factor Four
Lions, Donkeys, and Prophets—Oh My!

And when he was gone, a lion met him by the way, and slew him: and his carcase was cast in the way, and the ass stood by it, the lion also stood by the carcase.

—1 Kings 13:24

Before we move on to other donkey factors, I want to share a somewhat obscure example in the Old Testament. There is a story of an unnamed prophet in 1 Kings 13, and when I read it, I became very curious to understand the message. Sometimes, when we read something, it is good to reread it and then meditate on it for a while to fully digest the meaning. I encourage you to read the whole chapter on your own.

So, go ahead. Read 1 Kings 13, and I will wait right here.

[Patiently humming]

Are you back? Okay, good. Here is the story in a nutshell. The nation of Israel was divided into two kingdoms. There was the Northern Kingdom (known as Israel) and the Southern Kingdom (known as Judah). God sent an unnamed young prophet from Judah to King Jeroboam in Israel to prophesy. The prophecy was that a king named Josiah would be born to the house of David. This king would burn the bones of the priest who sacrificed at the heathen altar that Jeroboam had built in Bethel. This prophecy was to be confirmed by a sign.

This angered Jeroboam. He reached out his hand to command that the unnamed prophet be taken away, but Jeroboam's hand withered. According to the King James Version of this chapter, it literally dried up. Yuck! This sounds like a scene in an *Indiana Jones* movie.

By the way, the sign that the prophet said would happen also occurred. The altar was split in two, and the ashes that were on the altar were poured out. Signs and wonders often confirm the message. But don't get too caught up with seeking signs. A wicked generation does that (Matt. 16:4). If all you seek is signs, you will eventually end up discouraged. If we focus on the miracle, we will be disappointed when it fades away. If we focus on the message, we will not be discouraged because God's Word does not pass away. In this story, the sign authenticated the message for the king. The message is what was important.

All of this, of course, freaked out the king, especially the thing with his hand, and he asked the prophet to ask God to heal him. God did, and the king's hand was restored just as it was before. The king, feeling gracious after this display of mercy, offered the prophet a place to sleep, eat, and drink. He also offered a nice reward.

However, the prophet had been instructed by God not to stay in that place. He was told not eat or drink there either. He was even commanded to take a different route home. Wisely, the prophet obeyed, and he immediately left for home, going a different way.

In the meantime, an old prophet heard about what had happened. He tracked down the young prophet. He was able to catch up with him because the young prophet had stopped to rest. God had told the young prophet not to stop, but he did. I am sure he was tired. He was probably even hungry. In the natural, it is easy to justify why he stopped. It makes perfect sense.

Unfortunately, this seemingly harmless act of disobedience put into motion a catastrophic chain of events for the young prophet. The old prophet caught up with the young prophet and tried to get the young prophet to come with him. There are theories about this old prophet. Was he a true prophet of God? Was he a false prophet? I lean toward the latter. God used him, perhaps like he used Balaam, but he was, in my opinion, a false prophet.

The young prophet, to his credit, was adamant. He would not go. Then, the old prophet came right out and lied to him. He instructed the young prophet that by the word of an angel, he had been told to bring the young prophet into his home, feed him, and give him something to drink. Now convinced, the young prophet returned with the old prophet and enjoyed his generous hospitality.

And then the other shoe dropped. While eating together, the old prophet spoke the word of the Lord. This is what the old prophet said:

> And he cried unto the man of God that came from Judah, saying, Thus saith the LORD, Forasmuch as thou hast disobeyed the mouth of the LORD, and hast not kept the commandment which the LORD thy God commanded thee, But camest back, and hast eaten bread and drunk water in the place, of the which the Lord did say to thee, Eat no bread, and drink no water; thy carcase shall not come unto the sepulchre of thy fathers.
>
> —1 Kings 13:21–22

That had to feel like a setup to the young prophet. The old prophet convinced him to come by outright lying to him and then turned around and proclaimed a curse. It was time to go. After finishing their meal, the old prophet saddled his own donkey for the young prophet who left for home. On his way out of town, a lion met the young prophet and killed him. The donkey remained unharmed. And then, for some strange reason, both the lion and the donkey stood guard by the young prophet's dead body. Contrary to the natural instincts of these two animals, they just stood there.

The old prophet heard about the incident and went to the scene. He laid the young prophet's body on the donkey and brought the body back to his home. The old prophet not only mourned and buried the young prophet in his own tomb, but he also instructed his sons to bury him there upon his own death, with the young prophet. And thus, the prophecy was fulfilled. It was considered an honor to be buried with your fathers, and so in dishonor, the young prophet was buried in a stranger's sepulcher.

The events and the miracle of the lion and the donkey showed to them and to everyone involved the truth of the Word of God. Once again, a donkey helped carry the message, represented in the dead body of the young prophet. The old prophet, this false prophet, was now forced to admit and proclaim the same message that the young prophet, the man of God, had proclaimed. The word of the Lord against the altar in Bethel and against all the houses of the high places in Samaria would, indeed, come to pass.

What, then, is the lesson of this story? When we break it down to its simplest terms, the moral is to not deviate from the Word of the Lord. Not. One. Bit. While we have powerful women and men of God around us, we are also living in a day of lying prophets. They are everywhere. They are all over the Internet, they are all over the TV, and they are all over our churches. We must be vigilant.

We must read the Word of God to know and understand its simple commands. The command given to the young prophet was just that—simple. Yet he easily compromised. Once we understand the Word of God, we should see the contradictions of the false prophets, teachers, and preachers who do not truly believe the Word of God themselves.

Unfortunately, many people may see the contradictions presented by false teachers but want to believe their lies. We may want to believe them so badly that they become truth to us. This happens because those lies are nice, convenient, and comfortable. They tickle our ears. They allow us to do what we want. They allow us to satisfy our natural desires because they sound so good.

Face it. No liar is ever going to try to sway you by presenting an unattractive alternative to the hard truth. No, they will present something that looks good. The end result, however, is destruction.

When I think about this story, I find it sad that the lying, old prophet got to live and was able to be buried with the man of God at the end of his life. It is horribly sad that the young, unnamed prophet heard the Word of the Lord, faithfully delivered it to Jeroboam, saw the power of God break the altar, saw God wither and restore Jeroboam's hand, resisted Jeroboam's offer of hospitality and reward, and then after all that became deceived by the lying prophet. One bad decision led to his demise.

Yet even in this tragedy, I see God's mercy. I really do not think God sent the lion to kill the young prophet. God's warning was to protect the prophet. God knew what would happen. Although He didn't provide the details, God said to just go straight home. He didn't owe the prophet an explanation. Even though we don't always get to know the why, we should still obey. The lion was already there. The young prophet did not have to be there. His disobedience—his choice—put him there. Even though he was killed, God showed mercy by not allowing the lion to devour his body. The lion didn't devour the donkey, either.

And the donkey, carrying the body of the dead young prophet, delivered the message to those there that day. The message is for us, too.

It is also interesting to note that the lying prophet used a made-up story about an angel to deceive the young prophet. Even if he truly believed he saw an angel (but the Bible clearly states that he lied), since when does an angel trump the Word of God? If an angel does not trump the Word of God, why do we think a man can trump the Word of God? Yet it happens all too frequently.

> But though we, or an angel from heaven, preach any other gospel unto you than that which we have preached unto you, let him be accursed.
>
> —Gal. 1:8

We need to be wary of accepting the word of a Bible teacher who speaks lies. We need to be wary of accepting another's word just because it seems desirable to us. It was only because it seemed desirable to Eve that she listened to the serpent's words. Paul warns us about how easily we accept people's false ideas.

> But I fear, lest by any means, as the serpent beguiled Eve through his subtilty, so your minds should be corrupted from the simplicity that is in Christ. For if he that cometh preacheth another Jesus, whom we have not preached, or if ye receive another spirit, which ye have not received, or another gospel, which ye have not accepted, ye might well bear with him.
>
> —2 Cor. 11:3–4

The gospel is simple—we make it hard. However, there is an elegance in the simplicity that is in Christ. Don't follow alternate instructions. We have the Word of God.

Deliver it, like the donkey, but also follow it yourself.

Factors to Consider

1. Why is it important to obey God completely?

2. Have you ever been persuaded to do something that was contrary to what you knew was right? What was the outcome? What did you learn from that situation?

3. Which is more important, the message or signs and wonders? Why? Do all these things work together? If so, how?

4. How can we know whether someone is teaching us lies but presenting them to us as truth? How do we know the difference?

5. One bad decision can lead to a catastrophic chain of events. Has this happened to you? What did you do about it?

Factor Five

The Jawbone of a Donkey

And he found a new jawbone of an ass, and put forth his hand, and took it, and slew a thousand men therewith.

—Judges 15:15

We have spent a great deal of time talking about the role of donkeys. They serve as beasts of burden, carrying valuable cargo. In a spiritual sense, donkeys carry the prophetic message. They carry the Word of God.

Donkeys also are protective. When assigned to a flock, they are naturally aggressive against dogs, coyotes, or other animals that are bothering a herd of sheep or goats. I have heard that donkeys can even protect against a bobcat. In the last chapter, we read that a donkey kept watch over the body of a dead prophet, even with the lion that had just killed him standing nearby.

Donkeys are fascinating animals. In addition to all their roles, donkeys have been used to plow fields. Horses and cattle can plow fields, too. However, there was a very specific commandment not to use a donkey and an ox at the same time. "Thou shalt not plow with an ox and an ass together" (Deut. 22:10).

Why is this? Aside from the obvious physical differences and practicality, there is a metaphor here of not being unequally harnessed, or connected, with unbelievers.

> *Be ye not unequally yoked together with unbelievers: for what fellowship hath righteousness with unrighteousness? and what communion hath light with darkness?*
> —2 Cor. 6:14

The donkey, an unclean animal (remember, it had to be redeemed), was not to be yoked with the ox, a clean animal. Another idea comes from Jewish teachings, which equated plowing with a donkey to seeking knowledge from heaven (religious training) and plowing with cattle to seeking knowledge from earth (secular training).

Could this be what the 10th commandment warns us against in regard to coveting?

> *Thou shalt not covet thy neighbour's house, thou shalt not covet thy neighbor's wife, nor his manservant, nor his maidservant, nor his ox, nor his ass, nor any thing that is thy neighbour's.*
> —Exod. 20:17

We should not covet anything that our neighbors possess, even if they have a nice, um, donkey (sorry, I just could not do that joke). That includes not coveting their religion and education. Perhaps it is a warning not to listen to the prophets or leaders of other religions or schools of thought. It is certainly possible and an interesting concept and interpretation.

And that brings us to our next story. Nearly everyone has heard the story of Samson. He was a judge in Israel and a man of extraordinary strength. His nemeses were the Philistines, who were known to be strong, uneducated heathens. They were also uncircumcised, meaning they were not part of the Abrahamic covenant. Regardless of these differences, Samson wanted a Philistine woman for a wife. And that is just what happened. At his wedding, Samson presented his Philistine guests with a riddle, along with a hefty reward for those who could solve it.

> *And Samson said unto them, I will now put forth a riddle unto you: if ye can certainly declare it me within the seven days of the feast, and find it out, then I will give you thirty sheets and thirty change of garments: But if ye cannot declare it me, then shall ye give me thirty sheets and thirty change of garments. And they said unto him, Put forth thy riddle, that we may hear it. And he said unto them, Out of the eater came forth meat, and out of the strong came forth sweetness. And they could not in three days expound the riddle.*
>
> —Judges 14:12–14

Because this riddle came from a personal experience that no one else knew about, the Philistine men could not come up with the answer. They decided to threaten Samson's new wife in order to get it. And she complied. Before the sun went down on the final day of the contest, they revealed the answer to Samson. He was, of course furious and exacted his revenge on them. But before he did, he made an interesting statement.

> *If ye had not plowed with my heifer, ye had not found out my riddle.*
>
> —Judges 14:18

Some have interpreted this verse as some sort of sexual innu-endo. However, I believe that Samson simply said that they could not figure out the riddle on their own. In order to get the knowledge, they had to cheat. They had to use a worldly way to get the answer (plowing a field with a cow) and they couldn't do it by themselves (with their own cow). Neither was the answer revealed to them by God. They did not plow with a donkey. Rather, the solution was gained through their own treacherous, worldly methods. This interpretation is an interesting theory and a unique way of looking at it.

Regardless, the riddle set off a series of events of retaliation that escalated back and forth until it eventually led to the deaths of Samson's wife and Samson's father-in-law. Samson responded by killing even more Philistines, and the men of Judah eventually turned him over to the Philistines. Actually, I think they played right into Samson's hands as they were set up for a stunning jawbone-of-an-ass whupping.

> *And he found a new jawbone of an ass, and put forth his hand, and took it, and slew a thousand men therewith. And Samson said, With the jawbone of an ass, heaps upon heaps, with the jaw of an ass have I slain a thousand men. And it came to pass, when he had made an end of speaking, that he cast away the jawbone out of his hand, and called that place Ramathlehi. And he was sore athirst, and called on the LORD, and said, Thou hast given this great deliverance into the hand of thy servant: and now shall I die for thirst, and fall into the hand of the uncircumcised? But God clave an hollow place that was in the jaw, and there came water thereout; and when he had drunk, his spirit came again, and he revived: wherefore he called the name thereof Enhakkore, which is in Lehi unto this day.*
>
> —Judges 15:15–19

People love superheroes. Comic book movies are very popular today, and Samson seems a lot like a superhero. He faced a thousand Philistines on his own and prevailed, all the while wielding an unlikely weapon.

He was a hero, yet I wonder whether Samson really felt like one. He was all alone. His wife had been killed. His own people had betrayed him to the Philistines. As a judge, he lost his own country. He brought a lot of trouble on himself by his own actions, and he probably felt a little dejected—forsaken.

Have you ever felt that way? Maybe you feel all alone—even now. Maybe you are facing struggles and fighting battles. Some may even be of your own making. It happens. You are facing difficulties, just like Samson did. Although he may have seemed like a superhero, Samson was a fallible human being just like everyone else. In that way, he was just like you and me.

The key in situations like this is to not find the answer within yourself. Sometimes, we feel like we have to pull ourselves up by our own bootstraps. Instead, like Samson, we must take hold of the jawbone of a donkey that the Lord has provided. We all can probably identify with Samson in some way—capable of such strength and yet also capable of such weakness. We can find ourselves victorious one second and defeated the next. In all life's ups and downs, many of us are only looking for peace.

I think Israel just wanted peace. They wanted peace at any cost, and they were content with a false peace under Philistine dominion. They knew the Philistines ruled over them, and they did not want Samson making waves. I don't want to be content being ruled by my own Philistines. I am not happy being a slave to my lusts, my flesh, the world, and Satan. Neither should you. We should want to be set free instead of living life without making any waves.

To be honest, I really don't like conflict. I am not afraid of it, but I don't like it. I like calm. I like peace. I like it externally, but I also like it internally. But sometimes I have to shake things up. I have to stir up that gift that is within me in order to bring about change and a life of the peace of God and peace with God.

Wherefore I put thee in remembrance that thou stir up the gift of God, which is in thee by the putting on of my hands.

—2 Tim. 1:6

And she said, The Philistines be upon thee, Samson. And he awoke out of his sleep, and said, I will go out as at other times before, and shake myself. And he wist not that the LORD was departed from him.

—Judges 16:20

To make this happen, we need to be shaken and stirred. However, we have to be sure that God is with us. Scratch that. We probably had better make sure that we are with God. Yeah, that is the way it needs to be.

Samson fulfilled God's plan for his life by shaking himself and starting the process of delivering Israel from Philistine rule. As there would only be true peace in the land when Samson was victorious, so we only have true victory and peace with God and with others through the Lord Jesus Christ. He is our peace. Don't settle for false peace, don't compromise with the enemy, don't surrender your faith as Israel surrendered Samson, don't surrender your hope, don't lay down your Bible, and don't swap it for anything inferior. Don't settle for anything less than Jesus.

How does that relate to the jawbone of a donkey? Remember, donkeys carry the Word of God. Donkeys represent heavenly wisdom. The jawbone of the donkey represents speaking the Word of God. Our victory over the Philistines in our life will come when we use the jawbone of a donkey, speaking the Word of God, to defeat them.

Here is another point. Samson was at Lehi, which in Hebrew means "cheek" or "jawbone." It was a hill, or a high place. When the battle was over, Samson called it Ramath-lehi, which means "Jawbone Hill." And it was there that Samson found the actual jawbone of a donkey. There are a lot of references to a jawbone in this story, which is analogous to speaking God's Word.

The jawbone was God's appointed weapon that Samson found. God provided it, but Samson still had to take it. He seized the jawbone for battle. You may read your Bible, but do you actually take what it is saying and lay hold of it? We, too, must put forth our hands and take the instrument of victory and life—God's Word.

There is something else we need to consider. The jawbone was new (Judges 15:15). Had it been old, the bone would have been brittle and would have broken rather quickly in battle. Because it was new, it was strong. It was good for battle. Again, the jawbone is representative of us proclaiming the Word of God. We need to read the Word fresh and anew every day.

A couple of years ago, I was taken aback by a question a man in our church asked me. He asked, "What is God saying to you today?" I found myself stuttering and stammering. I realized that I really wasn't sure. The question was not a rebuke, but it sure felt like correction. It was. And I needed it. I needed to start listening to God instead of simply being busy for Him. I needed a fresh word for the day.

Yesterday's word was good for yesterday. I don't want to take anything away from that. But we can't live in yesterday. What is God saying to you—through His Word—today? As the jawbone may have seemed like an unusual weapon, so the Bible seems ineffective at best and offensive at worst to many. Even so, when used appropriately, it is effective in spiritual battle and a valuable part of the armor of God.

> *But he answered and said, It is written, Man shall not live by bread alone, but by every word that proceedeth out of the mouth of God.*
> —Matt. 4:4

Another point that is important to notice is that Samson was a Nazirite (see Num. 6), not to be confused with a Nazarene (a resident of Nazareth). This meant that Samson had taken specific vows of consecration. A Nazirite was not to touch a dead body, yet Samson defiled himself by touching the jawbone of a donkey in order to be victorious. In this action, we can see an example of what Christ did for us. He who knew no sin became sin for us. We are dead in our sins, but Jesus redeemed us (the donkey) and therefore is able to use us to proclaim His Word from our mouths (our jawbone).

After his victorious battle, Samson threw away the jawbone and then realized he was very thirsty. He cried out to God, and God caused a spring to come forth. While it may read like the spring came from the jawbone of the donkey, it actually came from the hill. Remember, Lehi means jawbone. The jawbone of the donkey would have eventually decomposed. However, the spring remained, as evidenced in Judges 15:19.

Samson called the place Fountain of the Crier. Living water came forth when he cried out to God. Likewise, Jesus is our Living Water. When we drink the water He gives, we will never thirst again. Our lives on earth will end. Our earthly bodies will decompose, like the donkey's jawbone. But the Living Water will remain. The things we say and do for Christ will last.

> *Let the words of my mouth, and the meditation of my heart, be acceptable in thy sight, O LORD, my strength, and my redeemer.*
>
> —Ps. 19:14

May the words that come out of our mouths—the jawbone of a donkey—be pleasing to Jesus and effective in our spiritual battles.

Factors to Consider

1. What is covetousness?

2. Have you ever escalated a conflict? If so, how did you get it back under control?

3. The Bible says not to be unequally yoked with unbelievers. Why is that so important?

4. What are some of your strengths? What are some of your weaknesses?

5. How do we get a fresh word from God each day?

Factor Six
A Colt, the Foal of a Donkey

Tell ye the daughter of Sion, Behold, thy King cometh unto thee, meek, and sitting upon an ass, and a colt the foal of an ass.

—Matt. 21:5

As I was finishing up my sermon series on "The Donkey Factor," which started on Palm Sunday, I was scheduled to preach on Mother's Day. Really? Another holiday? It was hard enough coming up with something new for Palm Sunday, and I wasn't quite finished studying donkeys. How could I tie in this important animal to moms? It sounded like a dangerous proposition. I had to tread carefully. I challenged myself to find it.

And I did.

Once again, it was something right in front of me the whole time, and I had never noticed it. When I finally did, it blew my mind. I couldn't believe I had never seen it before. My thoughts went back to something I had learned in a secular college class many years before, which subsequently helped me recognize something new. At least it was new to me.

61

As part of my bachelor's degree in management, I had to take some electives. I wasn't all that excited about this, and I originally enrolled in a class about the Civil War. I just wanted to get it done. I went to the first class and realized that particular course was not for me. I only had a few options left, and I found one—the Bible as Literature. I wasn't an English major although I had a fondness for both reading and writing. Because I knew the Bible quite well (or so I thought), I decided I would do okay. It was an elective, so I just needed to pass the course. I signed up for it as a pass/fail. In retrospect, I should have taken it for a grade since my professor told me I definitely would have received an A. She loved my writings and analyses, except she told me I was a little preachy at times. I have no idea what she was talking about.

Ahem.

Anyway, in that class, the writers of a textbook we used pointed out what they described as an obvious fabrication in Matthew's account of the Triumphal Entry. Their claim was that the writer of Matthew misunderstood the prophecy of Zechariah 9:9 and intentionally wrote two donkeys into the story—an ass and her colt—in order to make the prophecy true. The premise from this class was that it was a literary error caused by a misunderstanding of the Old Testament prophecy. The textbook claimed that the writer of Matthew's Gospel simply made it up because the other synoptic Gospels only mention the colt (Mark 11, Luke 19, John 12). The proof of this error was that Matthew was the only one who mentions both.

> *Saying unto them, Go into the village over against you, and straightway ye shall find as ass tied, and a colt with her: loose them, and bring them unto me.*
>
> —Matt. 21:2

I had never really given this much thought. Most (but not all) of the paintings and renditions of Palm Sunday show one donkey. But now that I was studying it, I wondered which it was—one or two? I really do not believe this was an error or a fabrication. Just because the other Gospels only mention the colt does not mean the mother donkey was not there. She just wasn't mentioned. What I love about the synoptic Gospels is that we find some stories unique to each book and other stories told from different perspectives. This helps us have a complete picture, much like the effect of recording different witnesses of the same event. Some details will be the same. Others will be different. When you put them all together, you can figure out what happened. You get the whole picture.

While both donkeys are only mentioned in Matthew, the other Gospels do mention other common factors. One is that the foal was still a colt, meaning it was not yet one year old. Additionally, it was a colt that had never been ridden. As I studied the characteristics of donkeys, I recognized that these were extremely critical pieces of information. Understanding this made the account in Matthew come alive and particularly relevant for Mother's Day.

Maybe you have already caught on to where I am going with this, but allow me to continue. Think back to some of the characteristics we have already learned. If a donkey is unsure where it is going, it might not move and appear stubborn. It just won't go. The colt was young and inexperienced and would not have known what to do if it was all alone, particularly with strangers. Furthermore, it had never been ridden. With the mother donkey leading the way, the foal would be sure to follow. You see, moms play an important role in determining the steps of their children, even with donkeys.

Aha! I had found my donkey Mother's Day message.

Moms will do a lot for their children. They will make a lot of sacrifices, including laying down their own lives. It is a God-given instinct. There are many stories, both true and fictional, that honor moms who do this. They are great and noble stories fit for amazing people. Moms are awesome!

However, I submit that a story just as great, if not more so, is about a mom who guides her child through his or her life. Moms who lead by example and moms who lead their children to follow Christ are the unsung heroes all around us today. We have them among us right now. We need to recognize them, and not just on Mother's Day. Moms are influential in leading our children to Jesus.

And I believe that is what happened in this story—the story of the Triumphal Entry. I believe the mother donkey led her foal to be in service for Christ. That is what I see. And while the other Gospels focus solely on the colt, Matthew gives us a glimpse of the awesome role of a godly mom. So let's talk about moms for just a moment.

Let's start with the word itself—*mom*. It is an awesome word that describes amazing women. These women are individuals who are able to do many things so very well. Quite frankly, I do not know how they do it. As I think about *mom*, I think of palindromes, words that are spelled the same forward and backward. That is a great analogy of a mom. No matter how you look at them, no matter what phase you are in life, no matter whether you are moving forward or going backward, your mom is there. She is steady. She is unchanging. Even when your world is turned upside down (and backward), your mom is *wow* to you (wow is mom spelled upside down and backward). We all have to be amazed at the strength, courage, and integrity of moms. Where does their strength come from? How do they do it?

While I believe the ultimate mom puts her faith and trust in God, I do believe there are God-given gifts and instincts that even people of the world find in moms. We see some great moms in Scripture. Although not perfect, Eve was a great mom (notice Eve is a palindrome). She was the mother to all mankind. Talk about the weight of the world on your shoulders. However, another great mom comes to mind. Her name was Hannah (notice Hannah is also a palindrome). Unfortunately, Hannah was barren.

One day, Hannah went up to the temple and prayed with great tears (1 Sam. 1:10) while Eli, the high priest, was sitting on a chair near the doorpost. In her prayer, she asked God for a son, and in return she vowed to give her son back to God for the service of the Shiloh priests. She promised he would remain a Nazirite (similar to Samson) all the days of his life.

Eli thought she was drunk and questioned her. When she explained herself, he sent her away and effectively said that her prayer would be heard and her desire granted. As promised, she conceived and bore a son. She called his name Samuel since she had asked the Lord for him. She raised him until he was weaned and brought him to the temple along with a sacrifice. The first ten verses of 1 Samuel 2 record her song of praise to the Lord for answering her petition.

The thing I probably most admire about Hannah is that she kept her vow to God. She followed through. How many times have we made a vow to God and then failed to deliver? It is better to not make a vow than to make a vow and not keep it (Eccles. 5:5). Hannah, a godly woman, kept her vow. She weaned Samuel and returned Samuel to God. He became a pivotal prophet to Israel. Change was coming, and everything came about because of Hannah, a godly woman who became a godly mother. She led Samuel to the Lord.

Moms, you may not fully recognize the impact you have on the world. You may not understand the width and breadth of your influence. If not, please know that you are vitally important. We need you. We need you to be godly women. We need you to keep your vows to God. We need you to change the world, but we also need you to raise children who will change the world.

However, like Hannah, many women are unable to have children. I have known a few people who were unable to conceive, and, like Hannah, their heart ached for children. Because of medical advances, some have since been able to have children. Others have adopted or had foster children. Some have never done any of these things, and some may choose not to have children, whether biologically or otherwise. I will not pretend to know the level of hurt, anguish, or emotion involved in all these circumstances and decisions. However, I know the pain can be real, and I am extremely sensitive to it because I have seen its effects on some great women.

Still, I am reminded of some examples in Scripture about non-biological moms. Matthew 12 records this conversation about the family of Jesus:

> *While he yet talked to the people, behold, his mother and his brethren stood without, desiring to speak with him. Then one said unto him, Behold, thy mother and thy brethren stand without, desiring to speak with thee. But he answered and said unto him that told him, Who is my mother? and who are my brethren? And he stretched forth his hand toward his disciples, and said, Behold my mother and my brethren! For whosoever shall do the will of my Father which is in heaven, the same is my brother, and sister, and mother.*
> —Matt. 12:46–50

This does not mean to infer that Jesus gave up on His family or abandoned them. He loved them. He died for them as much as He died for the world. He cared for His family deeply, and we will talk more about that in a moment. However, Jesus recognized and taught that the family of God goes beyond our pedigree and bloodline. We are part of the family of God. Ladies, you have an impact on our children, whether they are related to you or not. Again, this is not meant to minimize any hurt you may feel if you are unable to have your own children. But neither do I want you to minimize your importance or impact on other children. You are still needed. Desperately!

When Jesus was dying on the cross (John 19:25–27), He looked at His mother. Even in His own suffering, He was concerned for her. John was there, too. Jesus knew He was dying. He was taking care of some serious spiritual business. However, He also knew there was some serious natural business He needed to tend to. To me, it is like Jesus called a time-out on the cross. He was taking care of the sins of the world, but He knew that someone needed to look after His mom. It was probable that Joseph, Mary's husband, had long since died. Jesus tenderly provided for His mom at His death by asking John to take care of her. He established a new non-biological mother-son relationship between His beloved mother and His beloved disciple. And from that moment forward, a moment of love never to be forgotten, John treated Mary as his own mom. I am sure that Mary treated John as her own son, too.

It didn't erase or minimize the hurt, but it did fill a void and serve a valuable purpose. Something similar happened to the Apostle Paul. The last chapter of Romans is very personal to Paul, and there is a curious passage there.

> *Salute Rufus chosen in the Lord, and his mother and mine.*
>
> —Rom. 16:13

It is widely believed that Rufus was one of the sons of Simon of Cyrene, the man who helped Jesus carry His cross. While we don't know the whole story, we can see in this verse that Paul seemed to regard the mother of Rufus as his own mother as well. Because of his conversion, did Paul's own family disown him? Was his own mother deceased? I suppose we will never know, but this one little line in such a powerful letter to the Romans gives us a glimpse of the impact and influence of a godly woman, biologically related or not.

The motherly love of a godly woman can change the world. She can change the world on her own. She can change the world through her children. A strong woman can even change the world through other children. The mother of Rufus did. Unfortunately, our society has historically downplayed the importance of women in all areas of life. It is past time to correct that. Before we end this chapter, let me share an example and resource.

A fellow author and friend, Jamie Sandefer, wrote a book called *Love You from Right Here: A Keepsake Book for Children in Foster Care.* Like my book, it is published by Lucid Books. This amazing resource takes you through many of the emotions a foster child may experience when transitioning to (and from) a foster home. As the title says, it is a keepsake with a journaling section. It provides an opportunity for families to give foster children a piece of their history—their love—to take with them if they leave.

I first met Jamie when I was researching Lucid Books. She was a helpful influence to get me started publishing. Because I wanted to see the quality of their work, I ordered her book and was immediately impressed. Jamie is a stay-at-home mom and foster mom and is passionate about advocating for children in foster care. I loved her book so much that I purchased a bunch of copies of the second edition to give to a local foster care agency. Although many in our church have participated in adoption and foster care and I have been witness to the importance of these programs, Jamie's book touched my heart like never before with its final line, which is also in the title of the book: "I'll still love you from right here."

Wow!

I know this chapter has mostly addressed women, but this applies to men, too. Guys, I hope you've hung in there with me. We all have an obligation to raise our children, biological and otherwise, in the fear and admonition of the Lord. "Train up a child in the way he should go: and when he is old, he will not depart from it" (Prov. 22:6). It is such an awesome responsibility, a high and holy calling.

So from this Mother's Day message, the story of *Daniel and the Donkey Factor* was born. I actually wrote it the night before the sermon and shared it that Mother's Day at Hillside Bethel Tabernacle. From there, I set down a path to write my first children's book. I was nervous about it, but I am so glad I wrote it. The story changed a little during production, but the original thought that started from the example of a mother donkey and her foal birthed a powerful message that comes right from Scripture. I am so honored and excited to follow it up with this book.

In the next few chapters, we are going to apply the lessons from this book to the actual story, typology, and images in *Daniel and the Donkey Factor*. I hope you will find it helpful, particularly if you share the story with your little ones. Before we do, let me share one final story.

On that Mother's Day when I presented this sermon, we purchased some plush donkeys to hand out to all the moms present. I used it as an illustration and a keepsake to remind everyone of the message. Afterward, I had some left over, and I brought them home.

Because I bought them in bulk, many donkeys were in one bag. One of the packages had been opened but still had a lot of donkeys in it. I stored it in my office at home for future use because I was already thinking ahead to publishing a children's book. I thought they would come in handy as promotional items.

Not too many nights later, I came home to find our cat, Isabella, carrying one of the plush donkeys from the bag in my office into our bedroom down the hall. I followed her and looked under the bed where she went. To my amazement, I discovered that she had already taken several donkeys. She had rescued them from the bag and brought them to the bedroom to care for them. She can't have her own kittens, but she adopted the plush donkeys as her own. What a sweet example of the love generated from parental instinct, even for children not her own.

> *Pure religion and undefiled before God and the Father is this, To visit the fatherless and widows in their affliction, and to keep himself unspotted from the world.*
>
> —James 1:27

Isabella, the cat, saw the importance of helping the plush donkeys she thought were in need. Although she is not a biological mother, her motherly instincts kicked in. Those same God-given parental instincts are also in us. We are surrounded by a bunch of little ginnies and jackasses in our neighborhoods, churches, and communities. Many of them need to be rescued. Let's make sure we are leading them to Jesus.

Thank you, Isabella, for the precious reminder that we need to save the little donkeys.

Factors to Consider

1. Is Proverbs 22:6 a promise? Why or why not?

2. Name someone who was a non-biological parental figure in your life. How did they influence you to follow Jesus?

3. What does it mean to honor your father and mother?

4. Why should we be concerned with orphaned or foster children? What responsibility, if any, do we have to them?

5. How can we better honor women in general in our society?

Factor Seven
Daniel and the Donkey Factor (Act 1)

Long ago, outside the city of Jerusalem, a baby donkey was born. All the barn animals gathered to welcome this new arrival.

An owl asked from the rafters, "Whoo . . . whoo is this?"

"This," the donkey's father answered, "is Daniel."

As Daniel grew, he played with the other young animals in the barn.

One day as they went out to the yard together, the animals made fun of him.

"Donkeys sound funny," said the owlet.

The calf said, "They are dirty, too. Donkeys are unclean."

The colt replied, "Warriors ride horses because horses are better in battle."

"Yeah, what good are donkeys?" they all laughed together.

Joshua the lamb stood close by. "Please stop, everybody," he pleaded. "You are not being very nice."

So the animals started to tease Joshua too!

Daniel decided to sneak away. He was sad because his friends had hurt his feelings.

Back inside the barn, Daniel's parents could tell something was wrong. "Why are you so sad?" Daniel's mother asked.

Daniel replied, "Is it true that donkeys are unclean? Why are horses better in battle? Why does everyone, except Joshua, make fun of me?"

"Oh, Daniel," his mother said. "Let me tell you a story. Many years ago, God made everything and all of us to be different. We just have to find that special way we are to serve God.

"Donkeys are considered unclean under God's Law," she continued. "Yet He loves us so much that He made a way for us to serve Him. Did you know that prophets, priests, and kings ride donkeys? Donkeys carry very important people!"

"Really?" Daniel wondered. "But we sound so funny."

"Hee-haw," Daniel's father brayed. "Yes, Daniel, we do. But God once used a donkey to speak to a prophet. God can use anyone, Daniel. He can use you."

"How?" Daniel asked.

"One day, you will know. Until then, we will teach you and show you the way," his mother lovingly replied.

And they both did just that. Daniel learned as he grew big and strong.

Daniel and the Donkey Factor is written in four unique sections, or acts, that all build to the climax of the story. In the first section of the book, we find the birth of Daniel the Donkey. Although we are not given the exact time frame in the story, the event takes place more than 2,000 years ago. The story is considered historical fiction because while it is a fictional story, it is intertwined with the death, resurrection, and ascension of Jesus—a historical fact.

In the opening scene, the reader discovers that Daniel was just recently born. The other barn animals gathered around Daniel and his family with excitement. Just like today, everyone loves it when a baby is born. The owl even asks, "Whoo . . . whoo is this?" Anytime an owl is present in a story, that has to happen. It just has to. I mean, this stuff kind of writes itself, right?

But as we get to the next page, we quickly find that conflict begins to occur for our main character, Daniel the Donkey. He was out in the barnyard playing with the other animals. As kids and, well, let's face it, even adults sometimes, there was some teasing going on. You know, sometimes our kidding is just that. It is playful banter. However, teasing and kidding can be hurtful, even when we don't mean it to be. We need to be aware of that. Other times, there is actual bullying or physical violence. Because this is a children's book, we wanted to address this topic gently and carefully. These are Daniel's friends, but they are teasing him.

Regardless, this did hurt Daniel's feelings. They made fun of Daniel because he was a donkey. He was different. As we have learned, donkeys are considered unclean under God's Law. These other animals obviously knew that, and they teased Daniel about it. They pointed out his flaws.

The observant reader, however, will notice that the owl and horse are unclean animals, too. Many people who tease and put down other people are often aware of their own faults and put down others in order to feel better about themselves. Our own insecurities are often manifested in the way we treat others. I placed this subtle message in the book, but I want to specifically call it out here to make sure it is understood. We all have sinned. We are no better than anyone else. Period.

> *So when they continued asking him, he lifted up himself, and said unto them, He that is without sin among you, let him first cast a stone at her.*
>
> —John 8:7

Just as Jesus intervened to save the woman in John 8, Joshua the lamb stepped in to help Daniel. I used Joshua as a very important typology, and you probably already understand the symbolism. Joshua is the only animal character other than Daniel that is actually named in the story. We will find that Jesus is mentioned by name later on. However, He is the only human character named. I did this intentionally because the name Joshua is really the same as Jesus—Yeshua—in the original Hebrew.

While Jesus is the way we pronounce the name today, Jesus, Joshua, and Yeshua are all the same name, which means "Yahweh is salvation." We often think of Joshua simply as the character in the Old Testament who was Moses's successor. He certainly was that, but this is also technically the same name as Jesus in the New Testament. And so I used a lamb at this point in the story because he stepped in as a kind of sacrifice to help Daniel escape the teasing. He provided a way of salvation.

As Joshua deflected the teasing, Daniel took the opportunity to escape. The book's illustrator, Caitlyn Massey, did some wonderful illustrations to help capture the mood. There is a blue background around Daniel, his ears are drooping, and his tail is tucked. The teasing had an impact on Daniel. I remember when I first showed this picture to my grandson Henry he said, "He is sad." The amazing illustrations help tell the story.

Daniel was obviously hurt by the teasing. That can happen today, too. It is something that is true for both kids and adults. We all need to learn that teasing, even when done in fun, can be harmful and hurtful. We must be careful with our words and actions. When we see teasing and bullying happening, we need to step in and help stop it like Joshua did. This is an important lesson for both kids and adults to learn and remember. Unfortunately, we sometimes forget. I know I do. A gentle reminder is often helpful.

Daniel headed back to the barn, and right away his parents could tell something was wrong. It was obvious, so they asked him about it. When adults see  that kids are hurting, distressed, or bothered by something, we need to engage them in conversation. We need to find out what is happening in their lives. We need to talk. That is what Daniel's parents did. They asked him what was wrong.

In response, Daniel asked whether what the other animals had said about him was true. He heard something about himself, and he wanted to know whether it was factual. This was an important moment. Trust can be earned or lost at times like this. Daniel asked a direct question, and Daniel's parents took the opportunity to tell the truth. They gave him a direct answer. They did not lie to Daniel, but they did give him the truth in proportion to what was appropriate for his particular point in life.

Daniel's mother told him that donkeys are considered unclean, but she did not stop there. She followed up by telling Daniel that God loved him and that God made a way for donkeys to be used by God. They had value. Daniel had value. Daniel's mom did not get into the level of detail regarding sacrifices; however, she gave him the truth about himself, and she also set the stage for future conversation.

With children, it is critical to understand where they are in life. What is their age? What is their comprehension level? How much can they process and deal with right now? Daniel's mom knew what Daniel could understand, and she simply said that God made a way for donkeys to serve. She didn't get into all the details and simply left it at that, but there is more to come later. Without ignoring the question or lying, she set the stage for more instruction later. And it does come.

For now, however, she wanted Daniel to know that God used donkeys in very important ways. Although the teasing was factual on a certain level, there was more to the story. She told Daniel that prophets, priests, and kings rode donkeys. I used the literary tool of foreshadowing because Jesus is our Prophet, Priest, and King. This is a look back at what had happened in the past, but it is also a look ahead of what is to come. Donkeys carry very important people, and we are setting up the premise that Daniel will carry someone important, too.

Of course, no conversations about donkeys are complete without discussing how they sound. Daniel brought it up because his friends did. If donkeys sound funny, how can God use them? Daniel's father then referred to the story of Balaam. We have, of course, studied that story in this book. It is probably more detailed than children can comprehend, but they can grasp the basics. Balaam would have been killed if not for the donkey. The donkey carried an important message. So Daniel's father told a portion of that story. God used that donkey to speak to the prophet. God can use anyone. God could even use Daniel, a lowly donkey.

That brings me to an important characteristic of the story. Because *Daniel and the Donkey Factor* is a children's book, I thought it was appropriate to dedicate it to my grandchildren, Norah, Penelope, and Henry. All three of them are special to me, but Norah has some unique needs. She has Down syndrome. Although it is challenging, we try our best to make sure that it does not define her. She is Norah, and God can use her just the way she is, just like He can use Penelope and Henry. It is not about what we can or cannot do.

I wanted something a little different in the story of Daniel the Donkey, something we don't always see in other children's stories. In other books, we often find characters who are different in some way. Maybe it is a perceived disability or flaw that becomes their so-called superpower. We have Rudolph the Red-Nosed Reindeer, Dumbo, and others. I even remember another story about a donkey—Nestor, the Long-Eared Christmas Donkey. In all these stories, the protagonist is ridiculed for something that makes them different. Yet, they somehow overcome their difficulties and actually use them to save the day.

Yeah, this story is not about that. This story is about an ordinary donkey. It is about our ordinary children. This is about an ordinary you. God can use the ordinary. He is not concerned about your disability. He is not impressed by your ability. He just wants your availability. That is what we see in Daniel. He is just a normal donkey. He's nothing spectacular or unique; he is just an ordinary, everyday ass. God can use the ordinary for something extraordinary.

Daniel's parents recognized that and instilled those values in his life. They promised to teach him and show him. As a result, Daniel grew big and strong. What Daniel's parents did right then and there helped prepare Daniel for the next phase of his life.

Luke 2 tells us the story of the birth of Jesus. Nearly everyone is familiar with that passage. The last verse of the chapter was especially inspirational to me for the opening of Daniel's story.

> *And Jesus increased in wisdom and stature, and in*
> *favour with God and man.*
> —Luke 2:52

Even with all this type of instruction and preparation, there will still be ups and downs in life. Regardless, it is important to recognize the value of a good upbringing. Mary set a good foundation for Jesus. Daniel the Donkey's parents set a good foundation for Daniel. Likewise, we need to start laying that godly foundation for our kids when they are young. We must be careful how we lay it out to them. We can't just unload it all at once, but we must build that foundation of education and understanding. Our little donkeys need to know that God can, and will, use them.

Factors to Consider

1. Have you been the recipient of bullying and teasing? How did it make you feel?

2. Have you teased or bullied someone? If so, why did you do it?

3. How can we encourage our children to talk to us when something is wrong? What signs indicate that something might be wrong?

4. Have you ever stopped someone from bullying or teasing someone else? If so, how did that turn out?

5. Why is it important to be appropriately honest with our children?

Factor Eight
Daniel and the Donkey Factor (Act 2)

Months later, many people came to Jerusalem to celebrate a holiday called Passover. Daniel and his mother heard they were going into the city with their owner to get food for the party. While they waited outside the barn, two strange men appeared. They told Daniel's owner that the Lord needed to use Daniel and his mother.

This frightened Daniel. He did not know these men or what they would do. "Hee-haw, hee-haw!" Daniel brayed in fear.

His mother said, "Daniel, do not be afraid. These men are with a special man who teaches about God. He is kind to animals, children, and all people. I know we can trust them. Follow me." So Daniel bravely followed his mother.

Suddenly, a different man appeared. This man gently reached up and scratched Daniel behind the ears. He lowered His head and hugged Daniel's neck. Daniel was no longer afraid. He looked up and saw his mother looking at him. She gently nodded as the man sat on Daniel.

The other men led Daniel's mother toward the city. Daniel followed with the man riding on his back.

Jerusalem was crowded! People were all around. Some of them took off their coats and laid them in the path. Other people grabbed palm branches and spread them along the path. Daniel heard, "Hosanna to the Son of David: blessed is He who comes in the name of the Lord! Hosanna in the highest!"

Daniel's father had once told him of a king named David. "If this is the Son of David, He must be royalty, too," Daniel thought. Maybe a king was riding Daniel. He took every step carefully.

On the way to the temple, Daniel learned the man's name. "Look, it's the prophet," he heard the people say. "It is Jesus!"

Later that night, Daniel was so excited. He told the story over and over to the amazement of his friends. This time they did not tease him. They listened to every word. After talking for what seemed like hours, Daniel fell asleep and dreamed about his exciting day.

Our story picks up with a time of celebration. It was almost Passover, and that was very important. In the story, we are coming to the point where Jesus will ultimately be crucified. The events represented here in this part of *Daniel and the Donkey Factor* are commonly known as Palm Sunday or the Triumphal Entry. As I have previously stated, this story in the Bible was the genesis of my study of the symbolism of donkeys in Scripture.

Daniel and his mom were preparing to go to the city with their owner to get supplies for the Passover celebration. As beasts of burden, carrying supplies was part of their responsibility. It was a very busy time, not too unlike how we prepare for great holiday celebrations today. We take our vehicles to go to the store to get all the things we need. This was kind of like getting ready for a big party.

While outside waiting to go, two men appeared. As we know from Scripture, these men were actually sent by Jesus to get the donkey for His entrance into Jerusalem.

> *And saith unto them, Go your way into the village over against you: and as soon as ye be entered into it, ye shall find a colt tied, whereon never man sat; loose him, and bring him.*
>
> —Mark 11:2

As we have stated, I believe there were really two donkeys involved in the Triumphal Entry. Although three of the four synoptic Gospels only mention one, like the verse above, Mathew is quite clear there were actually two that day.

> *Saying unto them, Go into the village over against you, and straightway ye shall find an ass tied, and a colt with her: loose them, and bring them unto me.*
>
> —Matt. 21:2

Both Daniel and his mom went with the disciples. This is an important distinction. Daniel was a young donkey, a colt, which made him less than a year old. He had never been ridden before (see Mark 11:2). Remember, donkeys by nature appear to be stubborn when forced to do something they are unsure about. Rather than being a negative characteristic, this trait is often used to help bring comfort to other animals on a farm. If a donkey is there, it assures the other animals that they are safe.

While Daniel was understandably alarmed, his mother knew it was okay. At some point, she had seen and heard these men. Perhaps she and her owner had been around Jesus at other times. This man must have wanted to serve God, too, because he willingly complied when it was explained that the Lord needed to use the donkeys.

> *And if any man say ought unto you, ye shall say, The Lord hath need of them; and straightway he will send them.*
>
> —Matt. 21:3

Leading by example, Daniel's mom encouraged Daniel to follow her. He felt safe following her. And she led Daniel right to Jesus. This is an important concept I want to highlight because adults have an obligation to lead their children to Jesus. Parents, adults, teachers, church workers—all of us—have the responsibility to lead our own children, children in our church, and children in our communities by our example.

Left on his own, Daniel probably would not have gone. But because his mom led the way, he followed and headed toward Jerusalem. Then Jesus showed up, and I love the illustration of Jesus and Daniel meeting for the first time. Once again, Caitlyn captured the moment beautifully as Jesus gave Daniel a little hug.

I wanted to include this in the story to contrast Jesus's love for animals to Balaam's approach. Balaam was mean to his donkey. He beat her. Jesus, on the other hand, loves and is concerned for everyone, including animals.

> *A righteous man regardeth the life of his beast: but the tender mercies of the wicked are cruel.*
>
> —Prov. 12:10

> *Are not two sparrows sold for a farthing? and one of them shall not fall on the ground without your Father.*
>
> —Matt. 10:29

The men then led Daniel's mother toward the city, and Jesus, riding Daniel, followed closely behind. Some say that Matthew writes his account like Jesus is actually riding two donkeys. Unless Jesus was performing some trick riding like a circus acrobat or rodeo star, I don't think Matthew's account means that Jesus literally rode them both at the same time. However, they were together—mother and son—both serving Jesus in their own way. Without Daniel's mom, Jesus would not have been able to ride Daniel into Jerusalem. He needed them *both.*

Because of Passover, the city was crowded with people. As Jesus made His way toward the temple, the people took off their coats and laid them along the path. Others grabbed palm branches and laid them on the path. Why would the people do this? How did they know Jesus? What made them think He was a king?

I don't know how it all occurred, but I think riding the donkey was a major indicator that something special was happening. Most people would probably expect a great leader or warrior to ride in on a great stallion or have some other grandiose entry. However, it was prophesied that Jesus would enter Jerusalem riding on a donkey.

As we have learned, that was not unusual for kings in Israel. A lot of important people rode donkeys. One example already mentioned was when Solomon was appointed king. He rode into the city on one of his father's mules. Another example we have not mentioned yet was when Abraham was instructed to sacrifice his son Isaac. They used donkeys to travel to the location. They ended up going to Mount Moriah, which is the same location as the temple in Jesus's day. The story of Abraham and Isaac reminds us of God sacrificing His one and only Son. And in both stories, we see donkeys. Coincidence? I don't think so.

The Triumphal Entry was symbolic and also a prophetic utterance that needed to be fulfilled. It was not just because Jesus was humble. He was. But by riding on a donkey, He showed that He was a person of royalty. The people responded by their physical reactions and jubilant shouts of praise: "Hosanna to the Son of David" (Matt. 21:9).

This is important because Jesus was a descendant of King David. Jesus was born in Bethlehem because he was of the house and lineage of David. He was of the tribe of Judah. Because He was related to David, Jesus was royalty in a natural sense. The people were looking for a king to save them from Roman oppression. Could this Jesus be that person?

In the story, Daniel heard these words and made the same connection. Jesus was a king. And He was riding Daniel. But that is not all he heard. He heard the people say something else about Jesus. "And the multitude said, This is Jesus the prophet of Nazareth of Galilee" (Matt. 21:11).

Jesus was a king. That was true. We established that. However, He was also a prophet. He had that reputation and was known in and around the region for His prophetic words. In fact, many thought Jesus was a great prophet along the same lines as Elijah and John the Baptist.

> And they said, Some say that thou art John the Baptist: some, Elias; and others, Jeremias, or one of the prophets.
>
> —Matt. 16:14

Indeed, Jesus was those things and more. He was on His way to the temple. He was eventually on His way to offer His life as a sacrifice. Jesus is the only mediator between God and mankind (1 Tim. 2:5). That makes Him our Great High Priest.

If you study about the priesthood in the Bible, you will find that priests come from the tribe of Levi. It's in their jeans—I mean, genes (sorry, bad joke). The first priest, Aaron, was a Levite, and all subsequent priests were also Levites. Since Jesus was from the tribe of Judah and not Levi, how could He be our Great High Priest?

The book of Hebrews gives us some insight into this dilemma. The writer tells us that Jesus came from a different priesthood— the order of Melchizedek—that predates the Levitical priesthood. In fact, Jesus's priesthood is eternal. That involves some pretty deep theological teaching that is worthy of its own study. I encourage you to do that. However, for our purposes here, I simply want to lay a foundation.

Jesus is our Prophet, Priest, and King.

And He rode on Daniel for His Triumphal Entry into the city of Jerusalem. He rode in gentle strength. He rode to give His life. He rode to save His own. Just as the lamb was sacrificed to save the donkey, Jesus was coming to save us.

As we might imagine, this was a big day for Daniel. Afterward, he returned to the barn at home where he shared the story of his day with his friends. I thought it was important to show that some form of reconciliation had taken place. Even though his friends had once teased him, Daniel was still friendly with them. Making up with our friends is necessary and beneficial.

As Daniel regaled them with his amazing tale over and over, his friends listened intently. They did not tease him this time. They listened to every word. And they were happy for Daniel.

You know how it is when something great and exciting happens to you. You want to tell that story again and again. You want to relive it over and over. The excitement you feel after a once-in-a-lifetime experience creates memories that last. It creates memories you want to share with others. When it involves Jesus, what better story could we share? Do we have that kind of excitement about our personal experience with Jesus?

Daniel did. He told it repeatedly until he eventually wore himself out and fell asleep. I love days that end like that. I love falling asleep after an exciting day, fully exhausted because I had lived life to the fullest. Those are the great days.

It was a great day for Daniel. We have reached a high point in this story, but the story is not over. Some things are about to drastically change.

These things will also change Daniel. Not only that, but they will change the world—forever.

Factors to Consider

1. Why is it important to lead our children by example?

2. What are some practical ways we can lead our children to Jesus?

3. How is Jesus our Prophet, Priest, and King? Why is that significant?

4. Why is reconciliation with others important? Are there relationships in your life that need mending? What are you prepared to do about it?

5. What is the most exciting thing about your relationship with Jesus? Have you shared it with others? Why or why not?

Factor Nine
Daniel and the Donkey Factor (Act 3)

Several days later, Daniel and his mother returned to the city. Maybe Daniel would get to see Jesus again!

As they got close, Daniel noticed a change. Something was wrong. On a scary-looking hill were three crosses. Daniel heard some people talking. Some were crying. Some were even yelling. Soldiers were everywhere. Jesus, who had ridden Daniel just a few days ago, was on the middle cross. Daniel did not understand.

The sun began to set. Daniel realized he was walking through the shadow of the cross from high up on the hill. Tears came to his eyes. He was sad.

As Daniel followed his mother home, he noticed the shape of a cross on her back. Was it the shadow? No, it wasn't. As they got farther and farther away, the cross remained on her back.

Back home in the barn, Daniel asked, "Why were people mean to Jesus?"

Daniel's mother replied, "Remember when I told you that God provided a way for the donkey to serve Him?"

"Yes," Daniel answered. "I will always remember that story."

"Good. Now I will tell you a little more. Joshua the lamb stood up for you when your friends teased you. That is like what God did for donkeys. Because we are unclean, He allowed for a lamb to take our place.

"Today, you saw the very same thing happen for people," she continued. "They disobeyed God, so now they are unclean. Still, He loves them so much that He made a way for them to serve Him, too. Jesus is their Lamb. And you, Daniel, carried Him: the Prophet, Priest, and King."

Amazed, Daniel replied, "As we left, I noticed the shape of the cross is on your back. Why is that?"

Daniel's mother laughed and said, "It is on your back, too, Daniel. All donkeys have the shape of the cross. We carry the Word of God. The cross reminds us of that job."

And so Daniel thought about all these things.

We have come to the third act of our story. It is here that the conflict really begins to rise in Daniel's life. He had just carried Jesus into Jerusalem on Palm Sunday. Up to this point, it was one of the best days of his life. Our story picks up a few days later when Daniel gets the opportunity to return to Jerusalem. He was excited!

Unfortunately, when Daniel and his mother returned to the city, they quickly recognized that the climate had changed. It was almost as if a dark cloud had descended over Jerusalem. People were crying. Some were yelling. Roman soldiers were everywhere. It no longer seemed like a party.

Over the years, I have heard that it was the same people who cried "Hosanna" on Sunday who yelled "Crucify Him!" just a few days later. I don't know whether they were the same people. I think it was more likely the religious leaders. At the very least, the chief priests instigated the whole thing.

> *But the chief priests and elders persuaded the multi-*
> *tude that they should ask Barabbas, and destroy Jesus.*
> —Matt. 27:20

Although we may not know all the details for sure, the Bible clearly tells us the mood had changed. Something was different. Daniel could sense it, too. Everyone seemed to have turned against Jesus.

And then we read it. Jesus was being crucified. He had been betrayed, arrested, put on trial, and was now dying. As Daniel and his mother made their way through the city, they passed through the other side and made their way outside the city gates. They arrived at a hill called Golgotha.

> *And when they were come unto a place called Golgotha,*
> *that is to say, a place of a skull.*
> —Matt. 27:33

95

In the story, we don't get into all the details of the beating and crucifixion of Jesus. We do not actually see Him die. I think that might be too much for little ones to fully process. Because I want to be age-appropriate, without shirking away from the real meaning of the story, I give just enough details for parents and teachers to help fill in the gaps. I want adults to figure out how far the story needs to go with each specific child. We want them to understand, not be scared and traumatized.

Regardless, we can clearly tell that Jesus was on the cross. He was dying for our sins. This, of course, upset Daniel and his mother very much. There was so much that Daniel did not understand. It was confusing to him. As they prepared to leave the area, Daniel realized they were walking through the shadow of the cross.

As I studied the physical characteristics of donkeys, I came across some trivia I had never known. All donkeys have the shape of the cross on their backs. I discovered a book called *The Legend of the Donkey's Cross* that says the shape of the cross was formed on the donkey's back because it walked through the shadow of the cross. I, of course, do not believe that. However, I wanted to somehow incorporate that idea into the story. When Daniel noticed the cross on his mother's back, he wondered if it was the shadow. He quickly learned it was not the shadow because it remained as they walked away.

Why is this particular shape on the back of donkeys so important? Throughout Scripture, as we have learned, donkeys carried the Word of God. Daniel carried Jesus, the Word of God made flesh.

> *And the Word was made flesh, and dwelt among us, (and we beheld his glory, the glory as of the only begotten of the Father,) full of grace and truth.*
> —John 1:14

Many stories in the Bible involve donkeys carrying messages from God and messengers of God. Donkeys carried prophets, priests, and kings. Daniel carried the Prophet, Priest, and King.

So the symbolism is there. The cross on the back of the donkey is important, but it did not come from walking through the shadow of the cross. I believe that shape was there from creation and used symbolically as a message—the message of the cross that was foreordained from the foundation of the world.

> *But with the precious blood of Christ, as of a lamb without blemish and without spot: Who verily was foreordained before the foundation of the world, but was manifest in these last times for you,*
>
> —1 Pet. 1:19–20

As Daniel and his mother made their way home, we see that they were sad. Once again, the illustrator, Caitlyn Massey, displays the emotions so well in her drawings. I love this section of the book because the shadow of the cross goes through both pages as the donkeys sadly walk through the shadow.

When they arrived home, it was time for some reflection. It was time for Daniel and his mom to have a conversation about what they had witnessed. Conversations with our children, especially after major events, are important. What exactly did Daniel witness that day? Daniel's mother used the opportunity to go into a little more detail about the story of the donkeys and how God used the lamb to redeem them.

Because we are talking about death and sacrifice, I think it is, once again, important for adults to figure out how many details to provide their children. Daniel's mom referred to this command:

> *And every firstling of an ass thou shalt redeem with a*
> *lamb; and if thou wilt not redeem it, then thou shalt*
> *break his neck: and all the firstborn of man among thy*
> *children shalt thou redeem.*
>
> —Exod. 13:13

Daniel's mom explained that God provided a way for the donkey to serve Him. If the Hebrews wanted to keep the donkey, they had to sacrifice a lamb. God used the lamb to redeem the donkey. Instead of talking about breaking necks, Daniel's mom reminded Daniel about how Joshua, the lamb, had stood up for him when he was being teased. She used that story as an analogy of this principle of redemption in a way that Daniel could understand.

And then we bring the message home. Jesus was the Lamb of God, sacrificed for people. Our sins make us unclean. Our sins make us unable to be used in service for God. Therefore, God had to buy us back. And that is what redemption means—to buy back.

> *Christ hath redeemed us from the curse of the law,*
> *being made a curse for us: for it is written, Cursed is*
> *every one that hangeth on a tree.*
>
> —Gal. 3:13

We once belonged to God. Sin separated us. Therefore, He had to redeem us to get us back. That is what Jesus did for us. Just as God redeemed the donkey by a lamb, He redeemed His people by the Lamb—Jesus.

This whole section of *Daniel and the Donkey Factor* is about the cross. In fact, everything should be about the cross. Even before

Jesus, everything pointed to the cross. Everything after Jesus points back to it. Even our calendar is centered on Jesus. And so this section closes with the discussion of the cross. Daniel realized the cross was on his mom's back. He learned that it is on his, too. All donkeys have it, and he realized he was created for a very specific purpose—to carry the Word of God.

At this point in the story, Daniel understood the bigger picture a little better. I hope our little ones understand more about themselves at this point, too. It is a sad part of the story, but there is more to come.

There are things that still need to be resolved.

Factors to Consider

1. Why did the religious leaders want to crucify Jesus?

2. How do we teach our children about sacrifice and death? When is it appropriate to do so?

3. How do you explain the concept of the sacrificial death of Jesus to teenagers and adults? Is it different? How?

4. Explain why the cross is the central message in Christianity. Why is it so important?

5. Explain redemption. How did that apply to the donkey? How does that apply to us?

Factor Ten
Daniel and the Donkey Factor (Act 4)

About forty days later, Daniel, along with his parents, returned to Jerusalem. They went up a hill called the Mount of Olives. There were people there, including some men he had seen before. Daniel thought, "They were with Jesus!" He was excited. Could it be possible? Yes, Jesus was there, too.

Jesus walked over to Daniel. He gently scratched Daniel behind his ears.

Jesus then lowered His head and hugged Daniel's neck for just a moment.

Jesus stood up and gave Daniel a wink and a nod. Turning to Daniel's mother, He patted her gently on the neck, whispering "Thank you" in her ear.

Suddenly, Jesus began to rise to heaven. As He did,

He said, "Go and teach everyone the things I have taught you. Remember, I am always with you." And just like that, Jesus was gone.

Daniel had learned his purpose. Life was not always easy. But he never forgot the lessons his parents had taught him, especially the memory of his mother leading him to Jesus.

Daniel knew he had carried the King of kings, and now he carried the message of the cross. He knew that was a big job—a job meant for a donkey.

That was the donkey factor.

And you know what?

It is your job, too. Now you can go out and find your own special way to serve God and carry the message of the cross—just like Daniel did.

THE END

Act 4 is the conclusion of Daniel's story. In the previous act, Daniel and his mother witnessed the crucifixion of Jesus. Upon their return home, they discussed all the things they had seen and heard. Daniel spent the next few days trying to understand it all.

Although this may seem somewhat like a conclusion of sorts, the story is still hanging. There is still some tension that needs to be resolved. This last act begins about 40 days after Passover.

Then the eleven disciples went away into Galilee, into a mountain where Jesus had appointed them.
—Matt. 28:16

Daniel and his parents returned to Jerusalem and went directly to a hill called the Mount of Olives. As Daniel arrived, he saw some of the men he had seen previously, perhaps even the two who came to get Daniel on that original ride into Jerusalem on Palm Sunday.

Daniel was excited. He wondered if it was possible that Jesus was there, too. As before, I did not get into all the particular details about death and resurrection. However, the framework is there for parents to explain, once again, at the level appropriate for individual children.

And sure enough, Jesus was there. He greeted Daniel in the same way He had when they first met. He gave Daniel a hug and demonstrated affection and understanding. I wanted their last meeting to parallel their first, with a sense of completion.

However, as Jesus began to leave, He did one other thing. This did not happen before. Jesus stopped and said thank you to Daniel's mother. That was a special moment for me as I was writing it. I wanted a positive conclusion for Daniel. However, I also wanted a positive conclusion for Daniel's mother. I wanted to emotionally pull adults into the story, too. The intent was to stress the importance of leading our children to the Lord and that Jesus recognizes and appreciates it when we do.

We have talked about the parental obligation to lead and teach our children, who will follow our pattern and example, positive or not. Adults, we need to teach our children the right path. We also need to show them by example. Yes, we can change the world ourselves. I firmly believe that. However, we can also do it through our children.

I am so thankful for godly men and women who do both.

Women in particular do not always get credit for the things they do. Childbirth and childrearing are high and noble callings. They are. But ladies, you are more than that. You can do great things yourself. And you can also do great things through your children. We must not neglect that.

God has created both men and women for very specific roles and responsibilities. While not limited by these definitions, we must honor God in the roles and responsibilities He has given us. Raising our children is a monumental task for all of us. We do not lose our identity when we have children; we propagate it. So what are we teaching our children?

> *And thou shalt teach them diligently unto thy children, and shalt talk of them when thou sittest in thine house, and when thou walkest by the way, and when thou liest down, and when thou risest up.*
>
> —Deut. 6:7

I remember watching a recent Super Bowl halftime show. When it was over, there were a lot of thoughts about whether it was good or bad and whether it was appropriate or not. Without getting into all the details, one of the female performers brought her young daughter on stage to perform with her. I watched that mom lead her child into the same types of things she was doing.

To be completely honest, the style of music and dancing was not for me. It was not the type of show I enjoy. However, the performance skills necessary to do what she did were amazing. There was a lot of talent on display. Unfortunately, other things were on display, too. I did not need to see the skill set of her Brazilian wax technician.

There were some things I did not need to see, and neither did my son who was in the room with me. Now that is my opinion, and it is not meant to take anything away from the performance level or the expertise of the entertainers. However, was she leading her child in the right way by having her on stage with her?

I am not going to answer that for her. I am not going to judge her. I can't do that. However, we are all going to stand before Jesus. When we do, will Jesus look at her, will He look at me, and will

He be disappointed in how we raised our children? Or will He say thank you like he did to Daniel's mother?

> *His lord said unto him, Well done, good and faithful servant; thou hast been faithful over a few things, I will make thee ruler over many things: enter thou into the joy of thy lord.*
>
> —Matt. 25:23

These are the questions we have to ask ourselves. I know, we are good at judging others and criticizing their parenting skills. However, the real question comes down to me. What about me? What am I doing for my children? How am I making an impact for Christ?

We have to lead our children in the right way. Our future depends on it. Daniel's mother did. It changed her. It changed Daniel. It even changed the world.

As Jesus ascended to heaven, He gave some final instructions. If you look closely at the illustrations in the book about Daniel, you will notice that Caitlyn included Jesus's nail-scarred hands and feet. Remember, this is all about the message of the cross.

> *Go ye therefore, and teach all nations, baptizing them in the name of the Father, and of the Son, and of the Holy Ghost: Teaching them to observe all things whatsoever I have commanded you: and, lo, I am with you always, even unto the end of the world. Amen.*
>
> —Matt. 28:19–20

Daniel learned his purpose. He recognized that he was meant to carry the message of Jesus, symbolized by the shape of the cross on his back. Daniel literally carried the Word of God, Jesus, on his back, and now he carried the message of the gospel. Daniel learned that was his job. It was a job meant for a donkey. He did his part.

Now it is time for our children to learn their purpose. That is what I tried to drive home at the end of the book. Daniel, pointing outward to those reading the book, confirms this message: "It is your job, too."

It is not just the donkey's responsibility. It is not just our parents' responsibility. It is our responsibility. Donkeys are representative of us—all of us. That is what I hope we have learned in this book and in the story of *Daniel and the Donkey Factor*.

We all have to go out and find that special way we can serve God. We were all created with a purpose in mind. We were not made to just simply exist. God wants to use each and every one of us. He redeemed us. He bought us back. We just need to make ourselves available to Him.

Are you available to carry the message of the cross? I hope you are. I hope our children are, too. They are worth it. They are worth every opportunity we have to teach them, for God has a plan just for them. They need to live a life used by God. So do you.

That is the donkey factor.

Factors to Consider

1. What is the message of the cross?

2. Why is the resurrection of Jesus so important? What did it accomplish?

3. What are some examples in your life of how you are obeying the Great Commission?

4. Jesus is always with us. How does fully understanding that impact your daily activities?

5. How can God use an ordinary you to carry the message of the cross to your world?

Conclusion

The ox knoweth his owner, and the ass his master's crib: but Israel doth not know, my people doth not consider.

—Isa. 1:3

I hope you enjoyed this journey into the biblical world of the donkey. I know it was unconventional in some ways. Okay, maybe it was unconventional in a lot of ways. However, my intent was to stretch your thinking and understanding of what you already know and open your mind to new biblical concepts. I want you to always consider the Word of the Lord. I want you to live your life used by God.

In so doing, I also hope you recognize the importance and symbolism of the donkey. The donkey is an amazing animal and fascinating to study. I mentioned in the Introduction that when you see the value of the donkey, you will understand that being called a jackass is not so much an insult as it is a compliment.

I know, it is still hard for me to wrap my head around that one, too. Perhaps you should not go around calling people that just yet. There's no sense in needlessly ending up with a bloody nose.

Anyway, I hope you experienced the events of Holy Week, the ascension of Jesus, the stories of Samson, Balaam, and all the others through the eyes and ears of an important yet often overlooked factor.

The donkey.

My sincere desire is for my books and materials to be a blessing to you, your family, and your church. If you would like to purchase any of the books in bulk, please let me know, and I can help get them to you at discounted prices. Our ministry is not to simply make money but rather to provide sound teaching through quality books.

If you would like to use any of these materials in your church, we would love for you to do so. At Hillside, we held a special Palm Sunday service with *Daniel and the Donkey Factor*. We read the book to our children. We had special music from the Hillside choir. We had coloring pages and a coloring contest for all the kids. After church, we even had a petting zoo—complete with a donkey, of course—and a food truck on the church campus. Although the weather was a little uncooperative, we had a great day. We shared the story about the donkey, but we made sure the message was all about Jesus.

I was also privileged to have the opportunity to publish *Daniel y el factor burrito*, a Spanish version of the children's book. I partnered with Natalia Sepulveda, who translated the book so it could be shared with Spanish-speaking and bilingual children and families. That opened doors to share the message of the gospel so much farther than we could have otherwise. We are so proud of this endeavor.

And of course, Daniel the Donkey would never have come to fruition without the talents and abilities of Caitlyn Massey. Her illustrations helped bring the story and characters to life.

So many have worked on this so we could bring this message to you. Again, if you are interested in using these materials or would like to know more information, feel free to contact us through our website, www.thefactorbooks.com.

We would love to hear from you, and we would love to help you use these materials in your own church and community. Please let us know if we can assist you.

In the meantime, this has been a fairly exhaustive study. I don't know about you, but I'm pretty tired. We covered a lot of ground. We studied a lot of concepts. As with all things, there is a time to end it. There is a time to rest.

> *Six days thou shalt do thy work, and on the seventh day thou shalt rest: that thine ox and thine ass may rest, and the son of thy handmaid, and the stranger, may be refreshed.*
>
> —Exod. 23:12

Thank you for completing this study with us. It's time now to rest your ass.

Acknowledgments

When the idea of this topic first came up, my wife, Kathy, and I thought it was a joke. And now here we are with a children's book and an adult book both centered on a donkey. Who knew?

Beyond that, this book represents our third adult book. I am so thankful and blessed. I love writing and teaching, and I hope I can keep doing both for years to come.

But I can't do it alone. I fully recognize that. There continue to be so many people who influence me and are important factors in my life. This is not a complete list, but it certainly represents the quality of godly people I know.

Thank you, Jesus, for redeeming this old donkey. You willingly stepped in and took my place so I could be used by God. May I always carry Your Word as I look to You.

To Kathy, thank you for understanding me, although that is kind of scary. Thank you for encouraging me. Thank you for believing in me. Thank you for loving me. It is an honor, privilege, and joy to serve alongside you. I love you so much.

To my children, Breanna (and Cody) and Camden, thank you for supporting your old dad. I know, I tell a lot of dad jokes, but they are still quite funny. You know they are. I see you grinning.

To Caitlyn (and Nick), thank you for helping me bring Daniel alive through your amazing illustrations.

To my grandchildren, Norah, Penelope, and Henry, my desire is to leave you a legacy of life and love. I hope the message of Daniel the Donkey stays with you long after I am gone. Most importantly, I hope I have led you to Jesus. I want you to follow His plan.

My love and admiration also continue to go to my parents, Pastor Donald E. and Vickie D. Horath. The year 2021 represents 60 years of pastoral ministry for you. I find that almost impossible to comprehend. I am proud to be called your son. Thank you for believing in me.

To the congregation of Hillside Bethel Tabernacle, thank you for the opportunity to serve with you and for you. I love our passion for Jesus and our community. Let's continue carrying the message of the cross.

To the men and women of the Bethel Ministerial Association (BMA), thank you for your leadership, fellowship, and friendship.

To all those who have gone before, thank you for your faithfulness to the Lord. Your example to me was priceless. We will see you on the other side.

To Lucid Books, once again you knocked it out of the park. Thank you for partnering with me.

To all my social media followers and influencers, thank you for your likes, shares, and words of encouragement.

About the Author

Kevin P. Horath, author of The Factor books series, is a dynamic speaker and teacher who has served as Associate Pastor of Hillside Bethel Tabernacle Church since 1997. He has also worked as a healthcare human resources professional for more than 30 years. He holds a bachelor of science degree in management from the University of Illinois at Springfield. Kevin lives in Decatur, Illinois, with his wife, Kathy. They have three children, three grandchildren, two dogs, and one cat. In their free time, Kevin and Kathy love to sail on Lake Decatur. His goal is to help others find a spiritually healthy approach to life through the realistic, practical application of biblical stories, characters, and principles. Visit his website at www.thefactorbooks.com.

Other Works by Kevin P. Horath

Daniel and the Donkey Factor

Daniel y el factor burrito

The Pharaoh Factor: Living with a Hardened Heart

The Elisha Factor: Living the Double-Portion Life: A Devotional

CPSIA information can be obtained
at www.ICGtesting.com
Printed in the USA
LVHW080432120322
713192LV00009B/117